apart

a year of pandemic poetry and prose

Edited by
Courtney Bates-Hardy
and
Dave Margoshes

SWG
Saskatchewan
Writers' Guild

Published by
Saskatchewan Writers' Guild
Regina, SK, Canada

Library and Archives Canada Cataloguing in Publication
apart : a year of pandemic poetry and prose
edited by Courtney Bates-Hardy and Dave Margoshes.

Canadiana 20210222832   ISBN 978-0-9688451-7-2

LCSH: Covid-19 Pandemic, 2020-Literary collections.
LCSH: Canadian literature-21st century.
LCSH: Canadian literature-Saskatchewan.
CSH: Canadian literature (English)-21st century
CSH: Canadian literature (English)-Saskatchewan

Classification: LCC PS8237.C6 A63 2021   DDC C810.8/03561—dc23

Cover design and layout by Shirley Fehr
Cover photo by cek23©123RF.com
Printed and bound in Canada by Houghton Boston
Distributed in Canada by Radiant Press

Published by
Saskatchewan Writers' Guild
100-1150 8th Avenue
Regina, Saskatchewan
Canada   S4R 1C9

skwriter.com

The Saskatchewan Writers' Guild gratefully acknowledges the financial
support of SaskLotteries and SaskCulture.

The Saskatchewan Writers' Guild serves a membership
spanning the entire province of Saskatchewan in Treaties 2, 4, 5, 6, 8 and 10
which encompasses the unceded territories of the nêhiyawak (cree),
Anihšināpēk (Saulteaux), Dakota, Lakota, Nakota and Dené Nations
and the Homeland of the Métis Nation.

*Dedicated to the memory of all SWG members
we lost during the pandemic including: Don Kerr,
Geoffrey Ursell, Mick Burrs, and Doris Hillis —
all pillars of the writing community.*

2020

Mary Maxwell

d Covid Covid Covid Covid Covid Covid Covid Covid Covid Covid Covid Covid Covid Co

np Trump Trump Trump Trump Trump Trump Trump Trump Trump Trump Trump Trum

News News News News News News News News News News News News News News News N

Fear Fear Fear Fear Fear Fear Fear Fear Fear Fear Fear Fear Fear Fear Fear Fear Fea

CONTENTS

Editors' Notes

Poetry

Fiction

Nonfiction

Drama

POETRY EDITOR'S NOTE

Courtney Bates-Hardy

As I write, it has been just over a year since the pandemic started. Three members of my family have been vaccinated—my paramedic brother, my clinically vulnerable mother, and my nearly sixty-year-old father. I continue to work from home, as I have since the beginning of the pandemic, and wait for my turn.

I have lost family and friends over the last year. My grandmother died in the early months of the pandemic, not from Covid-19, but in a nursing home with no understanding of what was happening or why we had to stay away. A family friend and fellow poet died from Covid-19 just after Christmas. I watched his funeral on YouTube and dropped off baking for his family. I know I'm not alone in these losses.

Many of the poems in this anthology speak about loss. They grapple with grief and loneliness and the sheer enormity of this crisis. "How can I hold these numbers?" asks Raye Hendrickson, "each number a person." These are not easy poems, but they are necessary to the grieving process.

Inside, you will find many poems that were written during the first weeks and months of the pandemic; the fresh grief and fear palpable on the page. "You didn't know how easily / something so beautiful / could be broken," says Judith Krause in "How Beautiful It Is." But you will also find poems about the brighter moments, and all the ways these poets anchored themselves during hard times. Some have taken solace in nature: bird watching, hiking, or gardening. Others have found joy in baking or "Zooming" with friends.

Over the last year, I have watched friends get married on Zoom and cried happy tears. I've attended and hosted author readings virtually, many with authors I wouldn't have been able to see without travelling. I've baked loaf after loaf of bread and given them to friends, much like Maureen Ulrich in "Ode to Penelope." I've gone for walks and hikes and bike rides and swum in lakes and watched the seasons change.

It has been a gift to edit these poems; to have something else to focus on, to feel connected to others, to be comforted, challenged and, occasionally, to laugh and cry with the poets. These poems offer connection and consolation in our collective grief. They offer relief. They offer hope.

Grandmothers send love to their grandchildren from afar. A woman watches a little free library and all of the life going on around it. Mothers bathe and clothe their children for winter and a pandemic. Hope persists in these poems. Hope that the world will change for the better, hope that we will make it through, hope for the future. As Moni Brar reminds us in "Parental Wisdom", "it's a gift to feel whole / to see the world unhinge, then mend."

PROSE AND MANAGING EDITOR'S NOTE

Dave Margoshes

Editing this splendid anthology of work by Saskatchewan Writers' Guild members has been both a challenge and a pleasure.

One of the challenges was selecting the work going into the book from the more than two hundred submissions by almost one hundred writers. This is a curated collection – neither "first come, first served" nor "everyone into the pool." Saying "no" to some fine work was difficult.

The great pleasure was saying "yes" to some beginner and emerging writers. Of the seventy-four pieces of work in these pages (forty-seven poems, thirteen short stories, thirteen essays and a scene from a play), several are by writers appearing in an anthology – a book, not a magazine – for the first time, and a few being published for the first time, period.

All the writers in this book are SWG members – that was a basic requirement. It meant that a few lapsed members renewed, and we even got a sprinkling of brand new members. Not a bad way of increasing membership, but that wasn't the original idea, which was, simply, to showcase work by our members – and to evoke the texture of life during a medical crisis of unprecedented-in-our-lifetime proportions.

Guild members come from all over Saskatchewan – the cities, towns, villages and farmyards. And there are several in this book from elsewhere, Calgary, Vancouver Island, Ontario – even one from Alabama and one from Budapest. The writers are a diverse bunch, with an assortment of races, religions, skin colours and sexual orientations. There's a medical doctor, a few teachers, a sprinkling of PhDs, half a dozen current students or recent graduates of the University of Saskatchewan's MFA in Writing program and five former Saskatchewan poets laureate.

That diversity is reflected in their work but doesn't ever bog it down.

The one constant, other than SWG membership, is a reflection of life in a pandemic, when "normal" is a thing of the past and anxiety is a faithful companion. Through poetry, fiction (realistic, fantasy, comic and dystopian), literary nonfiction and drama, life in a pandemic – the current one, imagined ones and three stories that transport the reader a century into the past to the even-deadlier Spanish flu – is portrayed.

Some of these stories and poems are sad, some even heart-breaking; a few are funny. Most are thoughtful, carefully observed and insightful. What struck me most is the note of optimism that runs through them like a silver thread in a tapestry.

It was a hell of a year, 2020 was, a year, to borrow from the title of a popular novel, of living dangerously, a year of living *carefully*. But also a year of living hopefully.

It's our wish that readers of this testament to that memorable year will find hope in these pages.

- Dave Margoshes, with thanks to the sixty-eight writers whose work graces these pages, and the many others who submitted to the anthology but weren't chosen. And with thanks also to my associate editor, Courtney Bates-Hardy, and the support team at the SWG office, executive director Tracy Hamon, program manager Yolanda Hansen and publications coordinator Shirley Fehr.

THE YEAR OF US

Amanda Dawson

When it first began, you refunded our movie tickets and made popcorn at home instead. When I couldn't stomach the zombie flicks I used to love, you kept us safely ensconced in sitcom territory, or else dirty, absurdist humor that we could watch mindlessly for hours.

You kept the house stocked with fresh fruit and vegetables to keep us healthy and sustained our imaginations with visions of the far-off places we would visit eventually—someday soon. Iceland, New Zealand, Italy, Japan. We ranked and tallied our bucket list and you insisted it was better to save for a year anyway.

When we decided not to go camping as we had in years past, you shrugged and said that the mountains would be too crowded to have any real fun even if we had gone, and took me to every greenhouse in the city to find the perfect blueberry bush for the garden.

In the height of summer, you agreed to go for walks around the neighborhood at dusk, even though I knew you didn't really want to. The heat was bad and the bugs were worse, but I never told you how much those melting-asphalt evenings meant to me. When we turned west, the dying sun would settle on your head and even though I knew I was squinting, it would always turn your too-long hair into a red-gold crown. As if you were some kind of angel from the end of the world, and I would stare at you until you caught me looking.

When the snows came and the days shortened and my soul curled in on itself like a decaying leaf, the warmth of you only seemed to grow. When my eyes burst and tears streaked my cheeks, you would hold me until it stopped, and afterwards we would choose names for the children we might have and dream of the life that might be ours eventually—someday soon.

We lost a year of exploring the wider world and perhaps we will yet lose more. Of course this pains me, and I know that it pains you too. But the year we lost the world was also the year of us. The year we discovered that minute bubble of time and space in which only we dwell, and of which only we will ever know.

MID-MARCH 2020

Mary Maxwell

The troubled world has shut down.
Walking alone on deserted streets   each of us six feet apart
we cross over when someone appears on our side.
Fear drives us, fear of breathing the same air,
fear of sharing space, just in case.
The streets are silent, no cars, no airplanes above.
People peer out of windows as we pass by,
waving.

The waxwings have returned and are feasting on mountain ash berries
still swooping past the front windows, up into the bluebird sky.
The order of the natural world, undisturbed
undeterred.
The birds don't know there's a virus
don't know there's a spiked sphere that migrates and mutates
a creature that could take away our song.

Chickadees at the feeder pause to greet us, *chick-a-dee-dee-dee.*
The nuthatches upside down, peck away then toot their comical tin horns.
The March sun melts the reluctant snow, its leaving will be soon, it always goes
eventually.
Wind arrives and wakes up the tree roots, reminds them to think about
running the sap again, unfurling their leaves, their tender green flags.

For now, the birds flit and fly, nibble and squawk, store seeds in their hidey-holes.
Their precise stewardship and economy, their attention to the sphere of seed,
the bright blue sky that promises spring.

We return to the silence of the house,
update our wills, press pause, breathe
a new order, a new way of loving one another, loving the planet.

A CAUTIONARY TALE

Bronwen McRae

All green lights are hereby cancelled. Life is on a proceed
with caution only basis. Yellow. And red. Definitely red. Stop
when needed. Choose your time. Proceed with caution.
Step out from under
that sunny yellow glow, and go. Go
for a long stretch, a short stint. Go cautiously, curiously.
This life is weird right now. It screams of the need
for restraint. Go slow and stop.
Take a break. Take a nap. Check out
for a while. Refill your tank. Reboot your soul. It's okay to go
slow. It's okay to say no. This life is weird, right? This life
is weird right now. Smile today, because tomorrow you
might be masked. Mask up. Take cover. Take
your time. Today, green lights are cancelled.
Warning. Green lights will keep for another day.
Inspired days. Unfettered ways.

THE SICKNESS

Alice Kuipers

This isn't a fairy tale. There's no magic in the icy branches overhead, still and pretty as they may be; there's no happy ending waiting for me in the drifting snow, pillowed in soft beds along the riverbank beach. If I close my eyes, the memory of summer lingers. I was here with friends; Gina pointed at the water and laughed. "That pelican," she said. It seemed funny. If I close my eyes, I might die here, and so I keep them open.

I've gathered some sticks together and piled them up in a way that looks like they might catch fire; my shivering pale hand holds the lighter the stranger gave me earlier. "Worthless," he said as he dropped it at my boots, boots that don't fit well, and that protect me not from words, but from cold. Yet it penetrates. I pause and blow on my hands, I pull my lank blonde hair around my face, I shrug up my shoulders and tell myself the jacket I'm wearing is warm. There's magic in stories, but there's none in this one; the jacket doesn't get warmer, and the air I'm breathing blows dragon smoke before me.

Night is coming, as swift and seductive as the river clotted with ice.

I flick at the metal thingamajig of the lighter—I'm sure it has a name, everything does, but it escapes me. I'm waiting for a spark although my thumb's so cold it hurts. Gloves, such a small acquisition, so stupid to lose them. The flick, fail, flick, fail continues, but I won't give up hope; it's impossible to light the stupid thing, but eventually the corner of one of the crumpled sheets of paper I found in the garbage can flares. I'm a cheer team, vaulting on the snowy beach, look what I did, look at me!

In that light, I see my daughter, Jasmyn. Her soft, silvery curls, and her steady gaze. Her eyes were like the river in summer. It was not my fault, they said, The Sickness takes them all. But I was born to save her, and I could not. I held her hand, and now I see her standing next to Gina on the beach, holding her hand, the way I held hers. "Don't you think that's the best song of all?" she asked.

Gina said, "Sure."

I can't remember the lyrics. There were no pelicans in the music.

Jasmyn. I named her after the flowers that grew around the window in my father's house, being a breath of beauty in the small town of Romance, petals amongst the loneliness of the farm and the vast prairie, something to imagine when I closed my eyes. I was hopeful when I left at fourteen, even though it was too late, hitchhiking on the grid road; I'm hopeful now, even with all the scars. Gina says Hope should be my middle name. "It's Joan," I say.

The fire has not caught. The orange glow was haptic, and gone. Was it only this morning I found these five sheets of paper covered on one side with drawings by children? Dragons and castles and monsters. I took them from the recycling bin in the alleyway, an urge filling me; I wanted to write upon these pages, make something out of nothing, maybe tell a story, maybe write about Jasmyn and only her. I took those sheets and felt *I'm a writer today*. Then I spent many hours looking for a pen, hopeful whilst knowing that pens in the middle of winter in the middle of The Sickness were not likely. But the magic happened, and one poked out of the snow. Out of the snow—maybe this is a fairy tale after all, and the magic is in that pen sticking out of the snow, proof that I'm a writer, I'm a writer, I'm a writer. Although I'm sleepy, too, and so very cold.

How did it get so late? The sky is heavy now, the moon a brushstroke behind the clouds, and night stealthy upon me. I hear the dark water, but I can't see it any more. I stood in it under the full moon once with Jasmyn, we let go of many things together, until she told me her feet were frozen and she wanted to go home. I whisper now to the water of all the things I haven't done, the many lives I could have lived. Perhaps in one I'm a poet, doing a reading right now to an empty store, people watching on their screens from home. In another life, Jasmyn and I leave when I first hear of The Sickness and we find ourselves a cabin in the woods, no crumbs to follow, no witches, no gingerbread. In another life, we're with other people, laughing around an actual fire, playing music, looking for a pelican.

I screw up a second sheet and attempt to light it. I lost the apartment after Jasmyn died. The rental supplements that were designed for me, apparently, didn't come and didn't come and my landlord, once sympathetic, gave me notice and notice again. I think, technically, he wasn't allowed to evict me during this time, but what recourse do I have? My phone is long gone, and they never called me back anyway. Where does that money go, those supplements and those supports that are supposed to secure everyone through this? Do you know that the rich got richer through The Sickness? I don't know why, when I read of that wealth, I was surprised. I'm endlessly surprised; Gina says it's because I'm still a kid. Then she laughs. We're both so far from being kids. She grew up in foster care, apprehended at birth. They took her from a mother who was poor but bursting with love, and they left me with my monstrous father. We laugh about that too, otherwise we'd both be weeping. Who makes that sort of decision? How do they live with it? Gina tries to reconnect with her mother. Family is complicated, she tells me. Both of us laugh at that. Complicated is not the word.

Gina is not here with me, although I can hear her voice in the whispers of the shadows around me. In the glistening dark, I imagine big houses, those ones with foyers as you enter, space for no reason other than grandeur, windows that illuminate stairs, walkways that lead to Pinterest kitchens, tables groaning with food. Oh, to be this hungry; insatiably so, hungry for food, and for warmth, and for my daughter's laugh.

It wasn't easy. Having food for her took all my time and energy, and I have my fingers crossed that she never saw or knew how some of that money came. Perhaps in one of those lives that drift along this river, one of those men carried me into a family with many children, tables heaped with food, a roaring fire. Together we grew wealthy from The Sickness.

This paper lights. There's hope, right there, and I push my boots toward the small flame. Catch, catch, catch, I murmur, imagining in the flare the smiles of the children I did not get to parent. They let me keep Jasmyn, my only girl. I was on a good path, they said, I was doing better. It's true. I was. For her, I would do anything. I even attempted to gather back my sons.

I try to recreate a high; I've been successful at this sometimes, but the tremors and the fear often take over, and they do now. I want so much to feel differently, to be in the life where she's beside me, where together we're walking, holding hands.

And it's gone. The flame is gone. I try again. The third sheet of paper. In a puff, the childish crayon mermaid curls and burns.

There's my mother. She stands in front of me, in the light of the fire, and her gorgeous hair falls flaxen and soft, catching sunlight around her shoulders, just like Jasmyn's hair used to. The same green eyes, the same freckles. You're the reincarnation of my mother, I told my daughter; and I was hopeful when I said it that it was true and not true. My mother was love, she was hope, she was not here long. "Worthless," my dad called her, and when Mom wrote her goodbye, she put the words: *You are stronger than me, Princess.* For years, I've believed that. I think I still do.

Two people have frozen to death this winter. One was a thirty-four-year-old woman. Invisible. Four years older than me. I knew her name when I glimpsed it on the news, and I saw that the casualty of The Sickness isn't only those who die in hospital like my daughter.

I have the many lives that the river drags away. I have these words. I have a sea monster and I have a dragon on the two sheets of paper that remain. If I feed them to the fire, maybe I won't be here in the morning, frozen and red, my mouth open, but my words that I've written here will be gone. I'm afraid. Oh, I'm afraid.

I'm the matchgirl. I'm worthless. I'm still here.

I OPENED MY WINDOW AND IN FLEW ENZA

Holly Keeler

HOW BEAUTIFUL IT IS

Judith Krause

A week into lockdown, you lose
focus. Can't read. Can't write.
There is nothing on TV, nothing
but news you don't want to hear.
You move through your days
in silence, your nights quiet
as a stealth moth, its wings
engineered to deaden sound.
You only want what you can touch—
sticky dough you can fold
and shape, then bake into loaves
with crusts the colour of caramel.
Or clumps of humid black soil
to run your fingers through
before you drop in seeds
the size of hummingbird eyes.
Or the dark fur on your dog's back
glossy as a seal's pelt in the sun.
It will take months to recover.
You are like a fetus
growing in the womb, straining
to understand the voices
of those you will come to love,
muffled, as they are, by layers
of skin and water
and pounding blood.
You didn't know how easily
something so beautiful
could be broken.

ON THE LINE

Katherine Lawrence

I was on my cell phone giving clipped answers to a guy in the customer care department of an online store when I heard a baby cry in the background, a full-on howl followed a moment later by the nearer sound of a door closing. "Are you working from home?" I asked.

"I've been at home since the start of this craziness," he said.

Something opened in me. I wanted to ask where he lived. Canada? The U.S.? Was this his first baby? How many months old? I wanted to know if he was working at a desk in a bedroom, or from a table in a dining room, or if he had his own office. But I didn't dare ask another personal question. I'd heard the abrupt tone in my voice moments earlier. I'd even exhaled – through my nose – instead of accepting his apology for my thirty-eight-minute wait on hold.

He picked up where we had left off before the baby cried, and I heard a door close, and another one open. He asked for my address, my account number, and the reason why I wanted to return the stainless-steel espresso maker. I answered him in the voice that I reserve for my friends. I listened to the efficient tap of his fingers at a keyboard. I saw him sitting at a table in a bedroom with an unmade double bed at his back because the sound of that door closing suggested thin walls and choices as few as the rooms in his apartment.

I let my shoulders drop as I stood in my clean, quiet kitchen with a sleek phone held in my palm. I turned to face the window above the sink. The dwarf cherry tree in the backyard, a romance cultivar tagged Crimson Passion, was branched with fat, green buds. When had that happened? Yesterday? Last week? Each would soon burst into tiny white florets, then offer enough fruit for one deep dish sour cherry pie. On the other end of the phone line, a stranger offered me his service. And more. He offered me tolerance.

He spoke: "I'll need the reason for the return, please."

"I bought the wrong one," I said. "I need the next size up. I should have read the description more carefully."

"I understand. May I put you on hold again while I check the stock? I apologize for the wait."

I told him to take his time, I wasn't in a hurry. And it was true; I felt like I had all the time in the world for him. Soon he was back on the line asking for my credit card number, the expiry date, and the three-digit security code.

Our transaction was complete. He thanked me and I thanked him. Yet there was something about the exchange – not just the exchange of a four-cup for a six-cup – but my truce with this fellow and the someone who had calmed and soothed a crying baby.

I mailed the four-cup back to a warehouse in Mississauga. My new espresso maker was delivered to the front door a week later, as promised. I opened the box and lifted out the top, the bottom, the filter funnel. I held each cool, elemental stainless-steel piece in both hands before setting them down on the kitchen counter. I folded and flattened the cardboard. I read the instructions. The pot is a simple pressure-driven, stovetop brewer, unchanged since it was first designed over eighty-five years ago by an Italian named Luigi di Ponti. I carried the pieces to the sink. I rinsed the parts under hot running water, then dried each piece with a clean, white soft cloth.

I keep the coffee pot sitting in plain view on the back burner of my gas range. I brew a pot every morning, pour myself a cup, and move to my place at the table where I sit and read the newspaper. I don't think about the fellow from customer care anymore. Each new day offers another chance to refill and try again.

SORTING OUT ARMAGEDDON

Karen Klassen

while images of bodies
piled into mass graves
in Italy were broadcast worldwide,
Lexi and Brent
began to panic, not because they feared
death due to the lack of ventilators but

because the police now had
the authority in Nova Scotia to ticket
people for not maintaining
social distance

which meant
the military was going
to set up road blocks and turn
Canada into a police state

in a dream, God warned Lexi that
in three days' time looting would be
widespread despite mandatory curfews,
highway closures and lockdowns

together, Lexi and Brent banged up sheets
of plywood to cover windows from prying
neighbors and staged their dining room
table with Royal Doulton place settings
for four

they left prototypes of fake
inventions on the workbench
amongst scattered drawings and sketches
for the government to discover

they threw Kate Spade pumps and
Hugo Boss suits into black
garbage bags along with plastic
hangers and insurance policies.
tossed curling irons, face cream and
ski boots into suitcases

then a quick stop at Brent's mother's
to bolt three more sliding
locks to the back
of her front door

while Lexi stacked tins of organic black
beans and corn onto shelves in the pantry
and indoctrinated her elderly mother-in-law
about the impending doom

they dropped two thousand dollars cash
on the granite counter and told Anne
to be careful because the government
would be tracking
credit cards

they hugged her goodbye,
pried themselves from her frail arms
said they would come back
for her once it was safe

they roared off in their camper
leaving Anne to stare out the window
and sort out Armageddon
all on her own

ALONE

Ruth "Reno" Anderson

The silence was getting harder to take, and I did not know if I would ever get used to it. The scurries of creatures in the walls were the only noise I had heard for many nights, no music, no TV, no yelling, no talking. Only my silent sobs. I curled up in my corner of the room. The moonlight through the small window above my head lit up the door opposite the window, but little else. My legs cramped up from lack of use. My fever was gone. I had survived. Eventually I lay back on my pillow, covered myself up with a sheet, and fell asleep again.

I woke up when the moonlight changed to dawn. My stomach rumbled from hunger, and my head ached – no coffee for how many days now? No matter if it felt like eyes were everywhere whenever I ventured near the door. No noise, but eyes. Was there anyone else stuck in their fear too? I needed to find some food, some supplies, some people.

I dressed after washing with my last facecloth and pulled on jeans and shirt still damp from being washed in the sink. Barely dry. Not entirely clean. Who was there to smell me? I had cut my hair myself; now I pulled on a cap and tucked the ragged ends of my hair under it. The bones of my body were more obvious now, and I had to put a belt through my jeans to keep them on. Sneakers would be best, along with a jacket, the one with all the pockets.

With no electricity, cash would be my only currency, so I took four five-dollar bills out of the cookie jar and stuffed them into one of my top pockets. A knife went into my right-side pocket, unbuttoned for easy access.

Moving to my front door, I first put my ear to the space between it and the frame.

Silence. I carefully opened the three security locks, and eased the door open, gently turning the knob. The hallway was empty. I re-locked my door and turned to go down the stairs. A mouse scurried across the third step, and I choked back a gasp at the unexpected movement. I slipped down to the lobby, ears alert, and eyes moving quickly from side to side.

The door of my building was already ajar. It creaked slightly as I gently pulled it toward me, and I winced at the sound. I stood for a moment in the bright light. Not a cloud in the sky. Not a soul in sight. The windows in the three houses across the street were all closed tight. Not a glimpse of light in Sarah and Matt's house, or Mrs. Janzen's house for that matter either. I had no idea whether they were still alive, if they left at the start of this, or whether they had succumbed to the virus. Previous knocks on doors had produced no response, but that was weeks ago, before I got sick. I did not see any cars in the driveways. Mrs. Janzen's dog was not barking at my movement in her window as he used to, and even Sarah's son's tricycle was gone from its usual place in her front yard. I carefully walked to the sidewalk and automatically turned left, towards the shops, towards others.

My heart pounded as a tram rushed by at the nearest crosswalk. I did not see one face at a window: no evidence of passengers. And just as quickly it was gone. I turned to stare after it. Was it really there?

The sidewalk was empty. No mothers pushing strollers, no joggers, no school children walking with their backpacks to an empty classroom. Not a car on the road. My feet crossed the big street without pushing the walk button. No need.

Soon, the Rexall drugstore was on my left. The windows were dark. The doors were locked. I peered in, blocking the harsh light reflecting over my eyes with my hand on the dirty glass. The shelves were bare. No one restocking; no one cleaning; no one checking out items like diapers or hair dye or aspirin.

I hurried to the next building, the Safeway grocery store, expecting at least one or two people coming in or out. But here the door was not only gone, but smashed, as if a car had hit the frame and made it sag. I maneuvered my way in, walking carefully over the glass of the broken doors. While the aisles were unlit, enough sun came in that I could make out rotting fruit and smelly meat.

I grabbed one very ripe apple out of a pile of slush and bit into it hungrily. A box of crackers lay hidden from grabbers under a fallen sign down one aisle; a can of tuna left behind a post in another and, of all things, a box of tampons in the middle of the last aisle I ventured down. I grabbed my treasures and debated leaving a five-dollar bill on the empty checkout till. No need, this place would attract no one who would take it legitimately. The tuna I shoved into a pocket and found a plastic bag under the till for the rest.

I stood in the parking lot for several long minutes; tempting anyone to see me, to respond, to even try to rob me. But there was no one. Not a sound; not one human being tempted to kill me for crackers.

Next was the church, and I pulled out the heavy oak door, walked into its cool interior, and let the door close behind me with a swoosh. The cross at the front was stained glass, lit from behind by the sun outside, and beamed its blues, yellows, and golds into the centre aisle. I sat in the third pew from the front and gazed at that glass cross. If I was the only one left, would God still save me? I said a prayer and got up to walk out again.

As I turned, I sensed movement behind me. My hand went to my knife, and I sprung it open while withdrawing it from my pocket. I darted into the nearest pew and whirled back to the front of the sanctuary. There was a child, maybe age six or seven, a girl with a dirty face and matted red curls. Her clothes hung on her, and her shoes were untied.

"Hi," I whispered. No need to frighten her further, I closed my knife and put it back in my side pocket. "Hi," I said again.

"Are you a friend of my mommy's?" The small voice came out of her hesitantly, as if she had not used it much lately.

"I am not sure." My voice was not much better. Who was there to talk to? "What is her name?"

"Heather… Heather Kincade. My name is Chloe, and my mommy is dead, I think." Heather came out as hatha, but I knew what she meant.

I sighed. "Where is she?" I asked as gently as I could.

"In the back alley, I think. I ran away when the bad man came and hit her. Can I stay with you?" Her voice trembled, and she almost sobbed. "Are you a good lady?"

"Chloe, I am. Come here." I kneeled down and opened my arms to her. Chloe ran to me, put her dirty arms around my neck, and cried. "I miss my mommy so much."

"I know, I know." A child. Much like my eight-year-old Zabrina, who had succumbed to the fever that had wracked her body until it overcame her, and I had to dig a grave in the backyard of the house we used to laugh in.

The girl took my hand and guided me out the side door of the church leading to the alley, the sunlight hitting our squinting eyes. She pointed, and I followed her gesture.

Behind the dumpster was the body of a woman. I put my hand out to stop Chloe and walked slowly over to suss out the situation, looking for the predator. The woman was obviously dead, with a massive head wound and congealed blood. Young, early thirties probably, short red curls, and a wedding ring. Nice jeans, nice little boots, nice stay-at-home mom. Knowing there was nothing else to do, I rolled the body onto a large cardboard box from the dumpster and dragged her into the church yard. I positioned the box over her, hiding her from sightless eyes. Her pockets produced a driver's license: Heather Kincade, 315 Thomas Street.

I slipped the wedding ring off her finger and put it into one of my many jacket pockets, along with the license. I said a prayer, then turned back to Chloe, leaving her mother with the angels.

"Where do you live, Chloe?" I said, turning the child away from the sight of her mother.

In three blocks we were walking up the steps of a bungalow, nicely decorated front steps, with clever ceramic tiles saying 315 on the door, and a lovely painted mailbox. The door was open, and Chloe walked right in; it was home.

"I lived here with Mommy and Daddy, but Daddy had to go away to the hospital, and then the bad man made Mommy dead. So now can you stay here with me?"

Her tearful smile cracked my heart.

I thought longingly of my meal of tuna and crackers.

"Show me the kitchen." I said, as I locked the doors behind us. Chloe led the way into a white picket fence kind of kitchen, and I found a can opener in a cutlery drawer. Laying the tuna and crackers on a plate I found in the oak cupboard, I set it before the girl, and watched her eat. Was this life?

As Chloe devoured the simple meal, I poured us each a glass of water. It would do for now. I would explore the house later for possibilities.

No longer alone. I sat down and asked Chloe to tell me a story about her mommy. She would want the ring and license when she was older.

Together we would last until we didn't, but for now, we were not alone.

DO YOU HAVE PLANS FOR THE FALL?

Karen Nye

Who plans for the fall of civilization?
Who plans for the fall down the stairs?
Who plans for the fall of water
      before and after rivers?
Who plans for the fall of chins and boobs?
Who plans for the fall we all take
      from grace?
Who plans for the fall of economies, societies?
Who plans for the fall of the leaves
      of youth?
Who plans for the fall of all you know?
Who plans for the fall, this autumn?

ONLY LIGHT KNOWS WHERE TO FIND ME

Michelle Yeo

I have fallen out of time
        all I think of is cutting my hair

rabbits nibble unafraid—
            it's me who hides now
                    when my daily walk is over

I am lost inside the hours
            only light knows where to find me

my body is furred and musk-scented
            the plants start speaking
                    poetry lives in the ground
            the sheer porousness of everything

a crackling, like a radio between stations
            shimmering between the trees
                            in the clearings
            in the air between branches

a dog barks and breaks the spell

it begins again
            a crying cello for a pandemic winter

today I found a dead flicker
            perfect and still on the ground

head bent, listening

HEARTBEATS

Leona Theis

We are always, all of us, living and dying—squirrels and hares, lichens and algae, human beings and eagles. On a March afternoon in 2020, my friends and I snap into bindings and set off on trails groomed for Nordic skiing. It's a bright white day, blue above. Hares run circles around us. The trails we follow thread through a pocket of wild in the city, bordered three sides by freeway, train tracks, and buildings both industrial and residential, but along the southeast open to the river. Cougars have been sighted nearby, different times. Coyotes, foxes, moose. The South Saskatchewan and its banks afford a living, and they've learned to tolerate the clatter and screech of trains and the rumble of traffic. My friends and I stop a moment—carefully spaced two metres apart, a caution we're still learning—to watch a bald eagle as it hovers high above a pine. Three days ago we saw a squirrel bounding away from this same tree, *boing boing*, cartoon-like, brown against the snow, an easy target. We're chilling down now. We speed away not knowing if any squirrel's about to risk a run.

I stow my skis and drive home, the radio tuned to pop. A siren wail rips a hole through regular programming. Attention, please: two weeks of strict quarantine are mandated for anyone entering the province after international travel. We're heading into a tough couple of months, is how the thinking goes. Not so awful, really; an inconvenience. As usual after winter exercise, I feel freshly scrubbed inside and out. Strong. Ready.

> *The river is a wide ribbon of wild running through Saskatoon's built and tended cityscape. Plants in myriad variety thrive on the banks, animals move along it to and from areas of more natural terrain to the north and south. While scientists debate the interplay between habitat loss and animal-borne diseases, we know that nature in all its diversity is our essential life support*

system. Thriving natural landscapes are matters of life and death
not only for eagles, coyotes and hares, but for human beings too.
Urban rewilding efforts add pockets of diversity beyond what the
river offers. A space need not be large to be a wilderness. Native
perennials take root in spaces once covered with asphalt, flowers
bloom on rooftops, and all the bugs and beetles that help the world
compose and decompose move freely. A city full of life.
**

In July, my husband and I pack off to a lakeside cabin while my
sister-in-law quarantines at our house in Saskatoon. She's arrived
from Indiana to visit with family, most especially her mother,
Norma, who's gravely ill with Parkinson's. Norma: nurse,
professor, farmer, mother, grandmother. My mother in-law,
dearly loved.

On a calm morning, I circumnavigate Christopher Lake in
a twelve-foot kayak, a three-hour expedition. The white blade of
my paddle shimmers green underwater. The deeper I plunge the
blade, the more uncertain its shape below a veil of suspended
plankton. Eutrophy: too many nutrients. This lake, like so many
in the province now, is overfed. As summer warms, nutrients
build. Twenty-odd years ago when I began visiting, the water
here was clear well into late summer. Now, if I swim in August
and afterward hang my suit on the bathroom showerhead to dry,
my nose tells me I've brought the lake inside.

Around the north side of a small island I glide even with a
pelican. They come for the fish. I pass with care, my stroke as
quiet as I can manage. Floating there, the bird looks heavy and
weightless all at once, its body a bulk, the white wisps that stray
out at the back of its head, thin as whispers.

Four months into the pandemic, I still feel strong and ready.
But I have growing concerns about my elderly in-laws; about my
husband's brother, who lives in a group home; about the fault in
my husband's heart valve, which leaves him vulnerable.

Any lake worth plying with a paddle hosts its own fair share of
algae—in tangles, punkish wigs, and dot-sized drifters—along with

fish and frogs and pelicans, mosquitoes and the damsel flies that eat them. All this life, and more, relationships in flux, rebalancing moment by moment. Rebalancing until, that is, fertilizer runoff washes in year by year, supercharged storms sluice nutrients from the forest floor, septic tanks age and leak, and altered shorelines uproot the filtration system of trees and reeds and grasses. Then, as botanist Robin Wall Kimmerer says, "life adds up." The cycle of growth and death for algae accelerates. Week by week it settles to the lakebed adding yet more nutrients, devouring oxygen as it decomposes. Now that lakes are warmer longer, fish need ever more oxygen; and birds need fish; and so it goes. Remediation may be possible—there's hopeful action here and there—but it will happen over decades rather than years. Meanwhile, the growing season for algae is warm and long, and more so.
**

Norma's death in August brings a heavy weight of grief, and also a lift—for when a person gains release from a long and painful illness, there's reason to be grateful. Hers was a life well lived. Year after year she moved between country and city, farm and university—a four-hour drive with four kids in the car. Colleagues from the College of Nursing in Saskatoon remember her as a pioneer in her field. She built, from the ground up, a continuing education program for nurses across the province. In an era when doctors weren't known for recognizing common ground with nurses, she partnered with continuing education for physicians, reaching over professional borders and finding people willing to reach back.

For more than three decades, she was a dear friend to me, and we shared a wry sense of humour. Years ago she declared, "When I die, I want Henri Loiselle to sing at my funeral." In the mid-1960s, Henri was a student in the University of Saskatchewan School of Agriculture, where Norma's husband, Fred, was a professor. Henri's other *alma maters* were the University of Toronto Opera School and the International Institute of Vocal Arts in Chiari, Italy. For years he farmed in summer and toured in winter. Henri died in June, just two months before Norma, after decades of producing, as the obituary phrased it, "food for both body and soul."

Norma spent much of her final three years in a sunroom in her home, Fred and other caregivers attending to her needs. It's impossible to know how much she understood of conversations we had by her bedside. Did she, for instance, understand that her eldest child might soon have a date for open-heart surgery to repair his faulty valve? In that sunroom, the family gathers now to hold a virtual memorial joined by friends and relatives elsewhere on laptops, phones, and tablets. During the service, we listen to a recording of Henri singing, in his resonant bass baritone, "Take My Hand, Precious Lord." His rendition is humble and tender. Christian hymns were a part of my childhood, and still they carry me, body and soul, to a home place.

> *We are tuned for music. A mother's crooning to quiet a child might have been the first song, long predating speech. Neuroscientists document the chemicals the brain releases when we hear music, but more meaningful to me is what those chemicals conjure. Soothing music can ease the distress of a person living with a heart condition. Music comforts, amplifies emotion, offers release. It bonds us. It is, as neurologist Oliver Sacks has said, central to every culture, in work and play, joy and grief. Twenty or thirty different parts of the brain are involved in our response to music, far more than come into play for speech perception. The main purpose of music in prehistory may have been cohesion, community bonding. We are interdependent beings in all our ecosystems—familial, social, political, global, natural. Without each other, we're nowhere.*
> **

Fortunately I know nothing of the drama on the operating table until the surgeon calls to say my husband is alive and will be well. I'm relieved that as it happened I knew nothing of the tachycardia after they opened his chest, how the medical team massaged his heart by hand to calm its rhythm, all while making an incision on his inner thigh so they could run a catheter with an electrode up in order that, if need be—if his heart were to race into the danger zone again when all hands were busy with the surgery itself—they'd be ready with a jolt.

For weeks and days and hours I've reminded myself repeatedly that cardiac surgeons mend hearts every single day. Heart surgeons, after all, stitched a tiny piece of silk over the hole between the ventricles of this same heart when my husband was but five, and sixty years later that patch still holds.

Valve repair, like so many other essential treatments, is deemed "elective surgery." Across the country people are living and dying with chronic conditions that will, in this uncertain era, remain untreated indefinitely. But we've been lucky, threading the needle between the first wave of infections and the wave that's sure to swell come winter. The message saying we had a date arrived on the day of Norma's memorial. As I absorbed the news, I felt a rebalancing, a shift. Sixty years earlier, Norma had journeyed by train with her little boy to Rochester, Minnesota, for that dime-sized patch of silk.

> *The human heart clenches and unclenches a hundred thousand times a day, a relentless throb that possibly gave rise to the earliest musical rhythms. The beat a stethoscope picks up is the sound of valves closing, first the mitral and the tricuspid, then the pulmonary and the aortic semilunar. They open to let blood through; they close so it doesn't flow back. Or they ought to. When the tricuspid valve fails to close properly, there's a backwash. To supply the body with oxygen-rich blood, the heart must work harder. Over time, the right atrium enlarges. It's a complex muscle, the heart, operating within the complex system of the human body. When it falters, other organs—liver, kidneys, stomach—don't do their jobs well either. As fluid builds in the lungs, a person will be short of breath when speaking, walking, singing, even sleeping.*
> **

A few weeks before Christmas, my father-in-law is hospitalized and diagnosed with pancreatic cancer. The family brings him home to spend his final days in the familiar rooms where he's

lived for almost fifty years. His daughter drives once more from
Indiana and quarantines in a temporarily empty house offered
by friends. A son flies out from Toronto. Caregivers who grew
to love Fred during the years they helped him look after Norma
now shuffle their schedules to take "the Fred shift." One stops
by on her lunch break to cut his hair. Fred's children take the
challenges of his care in stride, and so does he. A few days after
Christmas, he takes his quiet leave, surrounded by love.

He was an open-minded man, inclusive, changing with the
times, early to adopt new ways of caring for the land. During his
memorial we listen to Henri sing "What a Wonderful World" as
we watch slides: Fred singing with his mates at a class reunion;
Fred dressed for Hallowe'en as a cheerleader; playing in a jug
band; holding his granddaughter. And we see him working: at
his desk on campus; planting vegetables with his grandson; on
the combine. An indoor man, an outdoor man. In wedding
photos, hair combed back, his skin tone changes from tan to pale
where his cap shielded his forehead from the sun.

Clearing his bookshelves later we find binders for every
board and committee, whether service club, church, or charity,
where he contributed time, energy and quiet wisdom. There are
stacks and stacks of binders, each one a record of a blend of
hope and action. Describing this gentle man to friends, I say he
spent much of his life answering the question *How can I be of use?*

*It's a pressing question: How can we be of use? For in the face of
runaway warming, the wealth chasm, biodiversity loss, systemic
racism, the birth and rebirth of outlandish conspiracy theories, the
idea of hope itself is under fire. Hope is passive, goes the criticism;
it has us watching from the bleachers, fingers crossed. Or this: hope
is nothing more than false optimism; it leaves us unprepared to deal
with the gravity of the challenges we've created. But despair, says
environmental scholar Elin Kelsey, will only further damage us. Yes,
we're in grave trouble, but if we don't hope, we don't mobilize. She
lays out an inventory of success after success. And author Thomas
Homer-Dixon takes hope apart and puts it back together: we need
to be clear-eyed about the gravity of our predicaments; we need to*

recognize the limits of what's possible at this late date; and we need the kind of hope that leads to action. What's the oxygen for that brand of hope? He has a one-word answer: imagination.
**

Saskatchewan and Alberta vie daily for the highest per capita tally of new cases nationwide. Vaccination stalls due to lack of supply. In January of 2021 there's an outbreak at Kinsmen Manor, home to my husband's brother and other intellectually disabled persons. Residents are restricted to their rooms, but my brother-in-law isn't awfully bothered by the isolation. He likes to watch sports and movies, play checkers on his computer, and listen to music. Pink Floyd's a favourite, AC/DC too. These, and birthdays, are his joys. In our family and to some extent beyond, he's the keeper of the calendar, which he carries in his head. He knows his nephew's about to turn thirty-one, and I expect that soon he'll ask what sort of cake I have in mind for the occasion.

The team at Kinsmen Manor do their difficult and risky work with care and dedication. Testing happens every Wednesday. Week by week, more tests come up positive. Most folks there have only minor symptoms, but two residents are admitted to hospital. Later, we hear the tragic news that one has died. For several weeks, my brother-in-law tests negative. On the day the nurse calls to say he's tested positive, she tells us one of his first concerns was to know how his friends were doing. He remains symptom-free. We visit with him every day by phone. He lets us know what he had for dinner, or makes a comment about the former president to the south, or tells us who he likes for the Super Bowl. But he isn't one for a long conversation. He'll turn on a dime to a cheerful, "Okay, bye." When he's two weeks symptom-free, the nurse calls to let us know he's in the clear.

The Broadway Theatre spelled it out on the marquee when all events to do with the JUNO Awards were cancelled last March hours before the kickoff: WASH YOUR HANDS. LOVE EACH OTHER. We can. We do. In the mid-1960s an Australian sea captain rescued half

a dozen shipwrecked schoolboys who'd been stranded for more than a year on the rocky island of 'Ata in the Tonga archipelago. They ranged in age from thirteen to sixteen. Before landing on the island they'd drifted for days, sharing rainwater they collected in coconut shells, one sip for each boy, morning and evening. Once landed, over time they grew a garden, harvested taro, played organized games, tended a flame, and raised feral chickens descended from birds long left behind by earlier inhabitants. They quarreled, and worked out ways to keep the peace. When one boy broke his leg, the others splinted it and shared his chores. They made music on a guitar fashioned from driftwood, coconut shell, and salvaged wire.
**

We are always, all of us, dying and living in webs of interdependence, negotiation, balance. Every part of every system—community, family, forest, ribbon of river, or twisting tale—negotiates a relationship with the rest. The boys on 'Ata understood that the more they pulled together the better their chances. Scale that up to larger and larger groups, however, and we divide, fragment, split off, compete. The reasons are myriad, deep, and complex—read the news any day from anywhere. But Earth is our common ground. Without each other, we're nowhere.

In February the province snaps into a spell of bitter cold. Nordic skiing's not much fun at minus thirty-nine. Instead, it's parka, wind pants, triple-thick mitts, goggles, and I'm bundled for a walk, west over one bridge, back east across another. The sun and its dogs are a triple-brilliant glow. The snow is deep and clean, white as the pelicans that will return to the river in April, floating near the sandbar, their bodies weighty, the wisps that stray out behind their heads, light as whispers.

FINAL DAYS

Moni Brar

What does it feel like?
Like you've swallowed the color grey.
Like your eyes could puncture the sky
and riddle it with grief-shaped bullets.
Like your lungs are filled with soot
and an ache as tender as a sparrow.
But what does it feel like?
Like you're clawing your way out of a black hole
filled with hot tar and memories.
Like you're straining to hear that beacon,
faint or fading, calling you home.

LONELINESS IN CHICKENS

Myrna Garanis

If you're a chicken, one really is the loneliest number.
Urban hen research spawned a bylaw: owners obliged
to keep at least three birds, preferably six,
to prevent *loneliness-related illness*.

I wonder how this rule applies to human coops,
knowing our tendency to pair off, to consider three's
a crowd, to avoid thirteen and ladders. It depends,
I suppose, on the hen house you grew up in,

whether there was a shortage of perches. Were
windows wide and low enough to scramble in
and out of? Any handy hidey-holes once life
proved complicated?

What's that unbearable squawking in the yard?
Six hens talking sense to themselves. Making you
lonely as you stand in front of the mirror. It reveals
only a third of what you're thinking.

Peer into its silverness. Aren't you yearning
for companionship? For a flock to come along,
summon you to their number?

DINNER WITH ANDREW CUOMO

Byrna Barclay

Every day, at exactly 5 p.m., Meredith (Birdy) and Russell James (Jock) MacBride take their supper into the den, turn on the TV, and settle in for an evening with excitable Wolf Blitzer in *The Situation Room*, who has no reason to smile, especially now; Anderson Cooper, whose face lights up like a neon sign on Times Square only when someone he interviews congratulates him on his new son; and finally Birdy's favourite, loquacious Chris Cuomo, who is the younger brother of the Governor of New York.

Today, wishing she could sit down for dinner with the warm and loving Cuomo family and listen to the brothers teasing each other, Birdy has whomped up a platter of spaghetti and Swedish meatballs, the latter a compromise since Jock prefers roast beef with mashed potatoes and gravy – every night if Birdy would agree to make it. He hunches over his plate, his pointy nose sniffing in disdain. "You know I don't like ethnic food!"

"Neither did Archie Bunker," she says.

"WHAT?"

"You like my Swedish meatballs."

Jock swivels his head quickly to look at Birdy as if she's Chicken Little and the sky has just fallen. "What did you say?"

"I'm not going to talk to you until you put in your hearing aids."

"I can hear everything you say."

"Eat your supper."

She believes Italians have spaghetti every meal, as a side dish if not the main course. If only she could ask Mama Cuomo!

Birdy MacBride fell like a robin toppled from its nest the first time young Chris Cuomo interviewed his elder brother on *Let's Get After It*. "I don't remember you being so warm and loving," Chris said to Andrew, or something close to that, right at the top of the hour, and the governor smiled that slow smile of his, a faint flush to his ruddy face. "Nice haircut," Andrew said, "but you need a new shirt. You look rumpled." Until that show, when she saw the governor for the first time and noted the familial hairline, Birdy was convinced that Chris wore a kinky toupee.

Then the host of the CNN show interviewed the governor, challenging him with his energy, at times seeming unable to stop talking himself, spittle leaking at the corners of his generous mouth. Birdy was sure he had a good set of dentures.

"Cuomo," Jock said. "He must be Jewish, one of those bright kids who never shut up in an effort to prove to parents, teachers, and rabbi that he was the brightest of the bright."

"They're Italian," Birdy said. As far as Birdy is concerned, in equal and opposite measure, the Scots suffer from emotional constipation when it comes to expressing their feelings, which has everything to do with their love of verbal scrapping. She should know, being married to one of them. "Crazy Scots," she mumbled.

"There are no people suffering from mental illnesses in Scotland," Jock said. "It's against the Law." This time, his hearing was selective.

"No, Italian," Birdy said for the third time since Jock didn't get it the first two.

He said, "Well, maybe a Jewish grandfather a few centuries back. These guys don't wave their arms and shout." Jock must have remembered their holiday in Positano. Every evening they took the two hundred steps carved into the mountainside down to the outdoor café where they were amused by the Italian families – so large in numbers – waving their arms and hands, shouting when they were happy with each other and hollering when arguing about everything important to Italians living on a mountain.

On TV, the brothers disappeared into their professions, the TV host maintaining his wide-eyed and questioning exuberance, the governor his poise and wisdom. "I don't think the governor fully trusts his kid brother to behave," Birdy said, "but I know what he's after." And sure enough, the governor expounded on the shortage of ventilators, the growing number of deaths, and the lack of federal response to the Covid-19 pandemic causing competition among governors, as if they were sibling rivals, seeking help from a tyrant who didn't care if their constituents lived or died. Although the governor was soft-spoken on TV, Birdy could imagine him raising his voice and the dome of his office with his booming courtroom voice.

Later, when Birdy watched on TV the gargantuan hospital ship anchor in the New York harbour to alleviate the shortage of hospital beds she swore she also saw the governor clad in armour and riding a white horse.

Every time she watched them, the Cuomo brothers could have been seated at their mama's table, the eldest serving his kid brother a huge portion of spaghetti. When Birdy was young, Italian men were known to cook, not just the Hollywood movie mafia who needed that survival skill when they hit the mattresses during feuds between families. If only Jock would learn to cook for Birdy. For over half a century Birdy has resented her mother-in-law for not teaching her darling boy how to make his own porridge. Some days, when reduced to shrieking like a crow by a pinched nerve in her back, forcing her to sit in her walker while stirring flour into Jock's beef gravy, Birdy vows to tell her mother-in-law in no uncertain terms exactly what she did to both her son and Birdy. Just wait until Birdy MacBride gets to heaven too!

Oh yes, one day Jock caved in and tried to learn how to cook a Sunday dinner, with Birdy seated in her walker beside him, telling him how to make stuffing, peel potatoes. Once the bird was in the oven, the vegetables in pots of water, Jock stood over the stove, his head swivelling while he stared at the pot of potatoes, then glanced at Birdy, then again at the potatoes. Finally, he said, "How can you tell when the water is boiling?"

Birdy didn't know whether to laugh or cry.

Tonight, Birdy cooked a prime rib roast and filled a casserole dish with baby potatoes, new beets, onion bulbs, and carrots, all drizzled with olive oil and balsamic vinegar. She asked Jock to put the dishes in the oven so she wouldn't have to bend her aching back, and took off for the den. When she returned to the kitchen, the casserole wasn't in the oven with the roast. She looked in the fridge, in all the kitchen cupboards, the microwave. No vegetables. She hollered at Jock, "What did you do with the casserole?" He looked bewildered as if she asked him what kind of cheese the man in the moon liked best. Then Birdy opened the dishwasher door, and there on the bottom rack rested the casserole dish.

"I didn't put it there," Jock insisted.

"Well I certainly didn't."

Then she hauled a jar of tomato sauce out of the pantry and cooked a pot of spaghetti.

Now, she twirls a length of spaghetti with her fork and tablespoon while Jock cuts his meatballs into small pieces.

"I hope the brothers are on tonight," Birdy says. "The world needs their love for each other to lift spirits – even if just for a moment." She needs them to make her feel better, to help her stay strong and well, their banter and affection for each other bringing warmth and smiles to Birdy and Jock, for each other.

The Cuomos fill her need for a large family. *Don't you ever wish we'd had more children?* It was Birdy who called a halt after the twin boys were born. Birthing babies was so easy she could have given him a brood, like kittens in a basket. It was the raising of children that was so difficult for an only child. She's always wished she'd had a brother, and now: just imagine, two like the Cuomos!

Since last March, Birdy has had groceries delivered by the little family-owned Lakeview grocery. She only leaves the condo to see her chiropractor, the gym in the building has been closed, and even her hairdresser has locked her doors. She's glad to stay home because it hurts to breathe when the temperature drops so low you can see the exhaust fumes whooshing out from cars and smoke from chimneys spiral straight up to a sky so white it looks sick.

Monotony has settled in with each day. Jock accepts the mask she makes him wear and uses the hand sanitizer at the security desk in the foyer. He goes wherever he pleases – his tailor, the pharmacy for blood pressure pills and Metamucil – but is sadly reduced to lunch with his cronies via ZOOM now that his friends' wives won't let them out of their houses. Birdy wonders how those women got such power.

When the news broke, with allegations of sexual harassment in the governor's office, Birdy cried, "I don't believe he'd do that!"

Jock said, "How fast, how easy we forget. New York was the first hit by the pandemic and Cuomo led the charge to save it. I feel sorry for him. If there's one accuser there will be others."

Every day now, every station carries the news of yet another woman speaking out, and it's getting harder to believe in the governor. Jock says, "He's innocent until proven guilty by the investigation."

"Maybe the women accusing the Governor are on a power trip," Birdy says. Having never worked outside the home, except as what she calls a "professional volunteer" at the provincial art gallery and a local theatre, no one has ever come on to her.

Jock says, "No one flirts anymore. It isn't safe." Maybe he remembers how their best man used to say to Jock, "Birdy and I are going upstairs now." And Jock would say, "Get me another Scotch first." And Birdy felt desirable but safe.

She says, "Being Italian and a politician, Andrew Cuomo buzzes everyone, sometimes on both cheeks like the French."

All Birdy has been able to devise from Google is that the governor was once married to a daughter of Robert Kennedy, and the Kennedys didn't like him because, they said, he was "no fun." Maybe his beginnings were too humble for them since his immigrant grandparents were so poor they only survived in America because a kind Jewish man gave them a tiny grocery store. Andrew's and Chris's father grew up to become Governor of New York. But maybe the old New York City rivalry between the Irish and the Italians infected the Kennedys – what does Birdy know since she is half Swedish and ¼ South Asian and only the good Lord knows what else?

All Birdy knows is that a shadow of sadness that belongs to a lonely man lurks behind his toothy, politico smile. There was something else in a gossipy rag about the wife and a polo player, which made Birdy suspect that she felt neglected when the governor worked nights six days a week to save the homeless, just as he does now for the people of his state.

Birdy feels like crying, as if she's lost a friend. But no, it was and still is more than that. Jock, that crusty old Scot, has never been one to show his affection for her in public. He had to be prodded and pushed by Birdy into hugging any friend, male or female. She sure wouldn't complain if Governor Cuomo touched her shoulder, her back, and if he took her face in his hands and asked for a kiss she'd, well, she'd just swoon. Yet, she remembers how in Capri, when she was young and leggy in a mini-skirt she was shocked and just a little afraid even with Jock holding her arm when the local boys hanging out on street corners not only whistled and hooted at young American women, they patted and pinched their behinds.

Now, Jock says, "It's probably just politics. "There's talk about him running for President in 2024. He's likely got a rival. What better way to take down an opponent than cause a scandal."

"Self-fulfilling prophecy," Birdy says.

"What's that?" He's wearing his hearing aids so he must not know the concept.

"You know, if a boy is told he's bad often enough he'll become a bad boy. Dean Martin looked like a Latin lover so everyone expected him to, well, do what he did when the shows were over, take girls to his hotel room. It caused a falling out with Jerry Lewis. Andrew Cuomo was voted – twice – as one of six sexiest men in the world by a trashy magazine."

"How do you know all that?"

"Magazines at my hair dresser's."

"Lord luv a duck, that first woman accusing him was abused before she worked for Cuomo, and still so young. This morning she spoke for four hours before the investigators."

"He said he was sorry, he feels terrible that he made her feel uncomfortable, and he will cooperate with the investigation. Inappropriate conversation –teasing!– is a long way from sexual harassment." It's getting harder to believe in the governor's innocence. The media no longer choose to show the most flattering photos of Cuomo, and in some, when he looks wide-eyed as if witness to an atomic bomb, he also looks too much like an old lecher.

Jock says, "Mentor or not, he shouldn't have asked her those questions."

"That's one of the things I love about you."

"What's that?"

"You never fished off the company dock."

Birdy is disappointed to learn that Chris Cuomo will not host his show today. Maybe he's too upset about his brother, who refuses to resign amid so many calls for him to step down, just before an election when the polls show fifty per cent of the voters still support him. She just hopes Chris hasn't been banished to his basement by a relapse of the virus.

And then, suddenly, leaning back and deeply into her red leather, Italian chair, Birdy MacBride watches her husband of sixty years disappear into a crowd of applauding personages. Her sofa chair becomes a folding metal chair facing a staged TV set made of café tables and chairs one usually finds in a village in Italy. Above the curtain a boxed light flashes: ON AIR. In the middle of the fake restaurant, seated at a table for four, is none other than Governor Andrew Cuomo.

Oh, oh, this is a TV show, called *Let's Go After Him.*

One lucky couple in the audience will be chosen to have dinner with Andrew Cuomo.

What if Meredith and Russell MacBride are the lucky ones?

What ever will she do?

What ever will she say?

And on TV too, for all the world to see and hear.

It is perfectly normal and perfectly acceptable for a young and leggy Birdy to doll herself up in fake fur hot pants, black patent Go-Go boots, a

Poor Boy turtleneck sweater, under a white leather maxi-coat. Her hair, of course, is cut in the finest lopsided Sassoon style, and her lashes are long again, her cat eyes beautifully defined with violet eyeshadow and black eyeliner, the Cleopatra look made popular by Elizabeth Taylor. Beside her, Jock-o wears his grey flannel wedding suit which still fits. Although he eats like an elephant he has never gained an ounce or ever gone on a diet. He's sporting a thick brush cut, a blue bow tie stuck on his Adam's apple.

And suddenly there appears before her, Perry Como singing *Hot Diggety Dog! Boom what you do to me, it's so new to me.* Of course, he doesn't look like a Cuomo, although Birdy has always been convinced that Perry Como was a relative and the Ad men had changed the spelling of the family name to make it more familiar to twentieth century fans.

What is going to happen next?

She sees herself seated beside Jock in the third row, an aisle seat. Now she's her good old self, wearing the pink chiffon dress with the silk poncho she had made for their sixtieth wedding anniversary, the party they had to cancel because of the Premier's pronouncement of limiting gatherings to only six people.

The MacBrides are called, a lump the size of a cherry erupts from her chest up to her throat, and tears spring to her eyes. She watches herself tremble yet rise gracefully, and take the arm of Chris Cuomo, who is wearing a tuxedo. He ushers her down the aisle towards the stage where Andrew Cuomo waits. He's wearing a bright red mask.

The table is set with dinner for four: lobster bisque, beet and feta cheese salad, lamb shank and Birdy's favourite dessert, lemon torte with whipped cream.

Who is the fourth person expected?

She hopes it's Mama Cuomo. She'll make her boys behave. Settle Andrew's hash good.

Instead, there she is, Birdy's long-departed mother-in-law, Mama MacBride, wobbling on low-heeled pumps, her hair all done up in a hairnet, two bright spots of rouge, a twitch in her right eye. She plunks the porridge bowl before her son. "Don't go to bed hungry," she says.

Across from Birdy, the governor smiles his generous smile, and says. "I'm the favourite son too."

There is so much she wants to tell Andrew Cuomo. How she admires him for his passion for helping the homeless and how when it snowed she rushed outside with her husband's old parka to a shivering young man who squats on the sidewalk in front of their high-rise condominium.

She will tell him he'll have to behave if he's going to run for the presidency of the United States.

He could save the world just as he did New York City.

He won't let Birdy MacBride and her faithful Jock fall sick.

Her time will come, but not today, not when she can dine with Governor Andrew Cuomo.

DÉJÀ VU

Bev Brenna

it's just like when I think about that cistern
black top bare beside the basement stairs
darkness dreaming dead dogs rolling
willful voices at the April moon
tearing it all to pieces

nights the house bays lilac with its grief
evaporating silver from the catchment
into handkerchiefs we've kept
in drawers that whisper precedents to this
and my eclipsed small terrors

spring is faltering and yet familiar
apple blossoms palming violet air
and breaking free where
elm trees rest their shadows on the lawn
and nightmares yield to dandelions

SELF-ASSESSMENT

Melanie McFarlane

We meet between the meat
and produce, unmasked
your laughter infectious
you touch my lips
I breathe you in

I bring you home
nestled behind my breasts
you hug my husband
kiss my kids

make me short of breath
make me hot
make me ache

Weeks later I wake, weary
freed from your affection

left with your afflictions

HOW I SURVIVED THE PANDEMIC

Sharon Butala

I'm now eighty years old, and a widow, living alone high in a condo overlooking playing fields, schools and a neighbourhood mostly obscured by giant, gloomy conifers. My "aerie," someone called it, as large black birds – crows, ravens, the occasional osprey – often swoop, disconcertingly, past my windows while I sit watching television, reading, or sorting papers to throw away or shred, so that my family won't have to when I depart for good.

One day, my life changed, not drastically but noticeably, when Covid-19 struck. Although, in my constrained world, I saw not a single sign of the disease, not wanting to be guilty of the illness or death of anyone else, I followed the rules: I went alone, once a week for groceries; I went for solitary walks every day, and when I met people I knew, kept my distance while stopping for a quick chat. Passing in our hallways, we older, single women spoke briefly to each other and stayed well apart. Most days I talked on the phone with friends who, as I often thought, were from *when I had a life*, now scattered across the country, and with family in other provinces. By the middle of the twelfth week, no one but me had been in my condo and I had not been in anyone else's.

I was relatively new to the city, had few acquaintances in it and fewer friends, and often felt that as a result, and because of my age and single- ness, I had already been to a moderate degree shut out of the normal, activity-filled world I'd once been part of. Covid-19 restrictions finished the job, so that there was nowhere left for people like me to go, and thus, we were alone almost all the time. My first reaction, though, surprisingly I suppose, had been relief.

This was because I lived in a constant tug-o'-war between my need to be *in* the busy social world, and my anxiety at having to engage with people I barely knew, or didn't know at all. But even an introvert has her limits, and the extra isolation soon began to unnerve me, even, faintly, to frighten me, although I avoided looking too closely at that fear.

Knowing social isolation is commonplace among the elderly, and having friends who, because they already had ailments, were in a worse situation than I was, I decided to quit whining and get a grip. I began trying to school myself in acceptance of my situation. I knew I had to find a peaceful existence, if I were to keep from banging my head against the walls or making hysterical late-night phone calls to total strangers.

I began to employ strategies to stay calm and to avoid thinking about the fact that I could not escape, could not travel out of it, could not visit people, go to the mall or the library or a reading, a meeting, any public event, not even a book club. But I had been a full-time writer for over forty years, and I knew how to use – even enjoy – long solitary hours.

I reread *The Brothers Karamazov*, all nearly a thousand pages of it, this time, though, studying how Dostoevsky had structured it, trying to see why and how it had so engrossed me when I was young, and in what way it was different from most novels written today. I started writing a suspense novel, a genre I'd never tried before and blessed the muse for the scene that one day popped into my head, out of which the whole book was developing – I worked diligently on it every morning. Normally the world's worst housekeeper, I began to clean house – inordinately. When all this failed, I became familiar with a dozen mostly inane TV programs, simply to pass the hours between when I finished writing for the day and going to bed. I decided, partly because the novel I was working on required it, it was time I learned about the murky underworld of vast *hidden* wealth and so, by ordering books on banking and the Panama Papers online, I learned how to set up offshore accounts, to move suitcases of cash, and to launder money.

I began to think how *nuts* the vastly rich were to love money so much since – guess what? – in the end it couldn't buy you love. But, that – I finally realized – *could* buy you prestige and privilege, and that *that* was in the end all the feverish acquisition of wealth was really about – not so much the diamonds, mansions and yachts themselves, pleasant as I'm sure they are. Hah! Why didn't I realize that a long time ago? What an idiot I am. Then I went back to my reading, to my suspense novel that was a constant enjoyment, and to my inane TV programs that, intermittently, bored me stiff even as I forced myself to keep staring at them.

But slowly, as I pondered and read and wrote, I began to re-find the rhythm of those thirty-three years when I lived with my husband on a remote cattle ranch and on our hay farm, when he went out each morning early to ride the cattle or irrigate or hay, and mostly, I stayed home alone and read book after book and began to teach myself to write.

Recalling those years when I was immersed in a literary universe and walking alone through the fields under the measureless, silent sky, I saw that I had not fully understood how precious that time was, how blessed I was to have it. Now, although I sometimes yearned for company, I began to find the once-stifling bonds of my prisoner-hood were fading as my perspective moved out to that greater, more luminous world, and with this, I saw the markers of ordinary time beginning, slowly, to dissolve.

I couldn't imagine living in such a world forever, but while it was happening, it was revelatory. I knew that out in the clamorous world I sometimes grieved for, people were sick, and many, helpless, without succour and in pain, were dying, but in my condo, for a too-brief spell, wonder prevailed.

NEW RULES

Bernadette Wagner

The child learns to suppress
love by withholding the urge to race
toward a friend who's passing by,
out for a daily lockdown walk
with parents and siblings, learns to stand
outside a window, hand pressed
against the pane while Grandma stands
inside doing the same, hands touching
each other's hearts. When the child blows
a kiss from the other hand, Grandma catches
the love with cupped hands and plants
it on her chest before returning
a love-flutter from her lips to the young one,
who mimics the catch, cupping love to heart.
When Grandma's hands stretch out as for an embrace,
the child starts for the door, but Mother's gentle hand
on the small shoulder is a reminder.
All they have known about showing
love outside their bubble has changed.
A bad bug wants to conquer the world. It's like
the killer games the older cousins wouldn't allow the child
to play at the family gatherings they all used to attend.

TEST

Lynda Monahan

the doctors can only measure symptoms
can't see the cracks in our walls
the elongated loneliness of the heart

swabs don't show
money worries or what to do
with the days of no work

they can't test for the unpaid rent
the kids all home from school
bouncing with boredom
or the teenager's slammed bedroom door

no antidote
for missing your grandchildren
whose faces you can only touch onscreen
or the lack of a friend to hold you
when worry steals you from sleep

and after the news at eleven
there's no test to show us tomorrow
when we finally turn out the light

CHILD OF THE FLU

Jason Heit

"Life keeps happening." Or so Joseph Eberle thought after his wife, Margaret, told him she was pregnant with their fourth child. That was in late March 1919, about three months after the flu that had taken Joseph's cousin, Katherine, and three others from the small farming community of Kaidenberg, Saskatchewan, visited their own home. Why it saved the Eberles for the end of its unwelcome visit to Kaidenberg, Joseph could hardly guess. But the extra weeks allowed the family to prepare their household and for Joseph and his father, Johannes, who lived on the adjoining quarter-section, to tend to their neighbours' livestock as both the Feists and the Werlingers took ill; thankfully, in that order and not both at once.

When the flu arrived at the Eberle home, it was the two youngest—Steven, four, and Helen, two—who first received its awful greeting. Margaret and Joseph had never seen their normally rambunctious toddlers so muted and weak. Within the space of a few hours both children were hauled to their bedroom. Helen drooped over a pillow, face-turned to the side, eyes heavy, just barely open; her body and spirit drained from the pendulous rhythms of fever, chills, and sickness. Steven was much the same except lying on his back with a wet cloth over his burning forehead. The two of them lay sick in their bed, breaking Joseph's and Margaret's hearts. Prayers were said and bargains made. And while Joseph was beside himself with worry, physically he kept strong—doing the farm chores, fetching water, fixing meals, washing dishes—as Margaret nursed the children day and night. It was Margaret's unfaltering belief that their children would pull through which strengthened his resolve.

"What makes you so sure?" He'd dared to ask her after their oldest, John, seven, also had taken ill.

"I know it's not their time."

"How?"

"I was told."

"What do you mean?"

Margaret spoke softly, her fingers gently tracing a path from Helen's brow to her cheeks with a cool cloth. "When I was a young girl, maybe, ten, my aunt, Rosina—they all said she had the gift...."

"The gift?"

"They said she could speak to your angels. And she told me, my angels had promised her, me and my children would live long lives."

"Ha..." Joseph caught himself, thinking of the miscarriage before John. No, this was Margaret's to hold onto, so he took her cool hand in his and kissed the top of it. "Nothing about your husband?"

She smiled. "Only he'd be a good man to me and my children."

"Our children." He smiled back at her.

*

Joseph continued on another day after Margaret took ill and became bedridden herself; and, although his father promised to come by to do the things needing doing, Joseph managed to finish the chores for the day. When he returned inside, the stagnant air of the house seemed to intoxicate him with its fever and sickness and he realized he'd better find his bed soon. But before he did, he stopped at the children's room which was lit in a soft, pinkish glow from an oil lamp atop the dresser. The Eberle children shared a feather bed, no more than four feet wide by five feet long; Joseph noticed the coverings on Steven's side closest to the wall had been kicked to the edge; with a flip of his wrist he unfurled the coverings which billowed and floated down upon the sleeping children. He noted Steven's lips still had a tinge of blue, while some of the colour seemed to have returned to Helen's cheeks. At the edge of the bed, on the open-side, was John, who opened one eye and mumbled what Joseph took to be, "I love you." He patted John's feathery brown hair as he braced himself against the wall. Then, as the fever swept through him like a hot July dust devil, Joseph staggered to bed and collapsed next to Margaret. A heavy darkness overtook him.

Later, he woke coughing. Each cough a knife sharpening its edge in his chest that left a slurry of blood in his mouth. He wanted to spit it out, wanted to turn his body to the side and let his head hang from the bed, but his aching body wouldn't allow it. Instead, turning his head to the side, he let the slurry pour from the corner of his mouth down his cheek and onto his pillow. It was then he realized that the light in the bedroom was wrong for morning, too much blue from the easterly window. He wondered if he'd been out for a day or several days; there was no one around to tell him, not even Margaret. He tried to call out but it hurt to speak. Surely, there was work he needed to be doing—feeding the animals, helping Margaret, the children. Where was Margaret? He prayed someone was there to help. A neighbour, his father. And then, the heaviness returned to his eyes, and he prayed for another day.

The next time he woke the room was dark. His chest ached but the knives were gone. He tried to move his body and although he could move his aching arms and legs in slow and clumsy arcs, he realized he'd get nowhere in the dark. He let the stillness of sleep embrace him and plant him front row in its dreamy theatre. And the dreams that came were so vivid, so powerful that they grew roots in his mind and stayed with him until his dying day some twenty years later. In one dream he saw his brother, Peter, dressed in white fur wearing a rack of antlers upon his head. Peter walked toward him menacingly, the tips of the antlers seemed to glow like embers as he approached. Joseph back-peddled and then turned to run, but found himself pinned in a corner with nowhere left to go. As Peter loomed over him, the antlers turned to great trees and Peter collapsed under their weight, and then it was he, Joseph, who came to his brother's aid, chopping the trees down to uncover his brother.

In another, he dreamt he was a baby calf in the midst of being born, desperately pushing his way towards the light. And his father was there, pulling him by his head and limbs into the world. Except, when he finally came into the light, he couldn't breathe; seeing the panicked look on his father's face, Joseph realized he was dying. Then, suddenly, his head was doused in a bucket of cold water and he saw himself, now from the outside, revived and shaking the water from his snout. It was that dream that woke him from his sickly sleep with a violent cry that brought Margaret not quite running, but hurrying as fast as she could to their room. When he told her about the terrible dream, he recounted to her how he'd once seen his father save what they thought to be a stillborn calf using the very same method.

"So, perhaps, you owe your father for pulling you through this awful sickness," she teased. "Or, perhaps, you just heard his voice. He was here earlier. He's been coming by to do the chores."

"Perhaps," smiled Joseph. Then, he wrapped his arms around Margaret, and rested his head on her bosom.

As it happened—and due to the help of much prayer, as Margaret would say with each retelling—the family made it through the troubling time without any deficits. In fact, in the weeks and months that followed, the Eberles' individual and collective battle with the illness, Joseph discovered within him a newfound gentleness. In his weakened condition, he'd relied on Margaret and young John in ways he'd never thought he would; and, without knowing it, Joseph, was displaying a joy he'd not felt since the carefree days of his youth—the warmth and gratitude he felt towards his neighbours and family flowed from that spring. And so when Joseph and Margaret joined together in that spirit of joy and tenderness, it was no surprise to either one of them that a new life would come from it. Except it nearly didn't.

*

By their own math, the child was expected at the beginning of December; so when an early November blizzard covered their world in snow and with it brought on Margaret's first contractions, a sense of worry infected Joseph and Margaret. What was most confusing, was that Margaret's pains were at their worst when she lay down on her side, quick and regular, and then, when she was standing or sitting, they seemed to lessen. This led to a series of sleepless nights that only exacerbated their worries.

After some days of it and not knowing what else to do, Margaret told Joseph to fetch his cousin's wife, Agatha, to help them bring their baby into the world.

Agatha confirmed their fears about the baby's position in Margaret's womb.

"We'll have to turn the baby," she said.

"Yes. Do it," moaned Margaret. Her face nearly pale from bearing the revolt inside her.

Agatha placed her hands low on Margaret's belly. She looked to Joseph, who was biting his nails, as he paced the floorboards at the foot of the bed. "Get her something to bite down on. This is going to bring on the contractions in a hurry."

Joseph raced to the door. "Like what?" he turned to ask at the last second.

"The wood spoon," said Margaret.

Joseph found the wood spoon in the drawer among the other cooking utensils, and as he shut the drawer he permitted himself a moment to look out the kitchen window and check on the children. As he'd hoped, John was minding the younger ones, pulling them on the sled Joseph had made from an old ladder and sheets of tin metal. He closed the drawer and returned to Margaret, wood spoon in hand.

As Agatha worked her hands into Margaret's belly, Margaret clenched the spoon with a deep bite pulling the corners of her mouth back towards her ears, while her fingernails sliced through the hard callous of Joseph's palm. The adjustments continued on for what seemed to be a small eternity, and when Agatha finished the baby had turned; and, although the contractions had quickened, the desperateness that had clouded the small bedroom lifted some.

Margaret wiped a tangle of brown hair from her brow and finding a certain stillness, turned to Joseph and said: "The children haven't eaten in hours." Then, quite suddenly, like thunder crashing in the summer sky, "Make them food!" she roared.

Taking his leave, Joseph busied himself in the kitchen—boiling eggs and frying potato pancakes on the wood burning stove—while Margaret's cries resonated through the thin walls of the home. With the food plated, he called the children in from outside; Steven and Helen wore fresh smiles as they entered from the cold, while John kicked off his boots. "Watch out for the little ones," Joseph warned him.

"That's all I do." John scowled.

"Listen…" And before Joseph could tell John that it was his responsibility to help with the children when their mother couldn't, Margaret cried out from pain and effort.

The children stared at him and he could see Helen's eyes begin to tear.

"No, no," he said. "Papa's made lunch for you. Sit. It's time to eat."

He brushed the tears from his daughter's cheeks with the cuff of his long shirt sleeve and set her on the bench next to the table. John and Steven took their places at the table as Joseph rubbed Helen's back, doing his best to soothe her worries. From the bedroom, Agatha could be heard asking Margaret for one last push. Then, a low moan.

"Stay here," said Joseph to the children. He returned to Margaret and Agatha.

"Good. Good," said Agatha. "Here it comes. One more."

As Joseph entered the room, Margaret collapsed to her back with an exhausted snort. Agatha pulled the small runt of a baby from its mother. "A boy!" she exclaimed.

In the next breath, she was quiet; she shifted the baby, cradling him face down in her left arm and carefully smacked his bottom. There was no cry, no breath. She smacked it again, a little harder than before, but with the same result. Blood poured from the baby's mouth. "Something's wrong." Opening the jaw, Agatha ran her pinky finger like a hook along the baby's cheek and cleared more blood from his mouth. She smacked the baby again but still he refused to breathe.

"Oh, God! Do something, Joseph!" cried Margaret.

Agatha offered Joseph the baby but without thinking he shook his head and turned for the bedroom door. The children had gathered there and he brushed them aside as he dashed toward the kitchen where his empty hand caught the handle of a metal bucket next to the cupboard; he continued out the door in his stocking feet to the well nearly forty feet from the house. There, he kicked aside the wooden cover set over the mouth of the bore well, then ran a hitch knot around the bucket's handle and let it fall into the darkness. The bucket pulled the rope through his hands until he heard it splash water; he tightened his grip on the rope, looping it once around his forearm as the bucket filled below. Then, after the bucket sank and the rope tightened around his arm, he began pulling it up with sweeping arm-over-arm strides. 'Do something. Do something.' Margaret's words tumbled in his mind. Holding the bucket at his chest he ran for the open door. Each step too slow: with the heavy snow, his feet numb and the water spilling onto his chest. What's more, he hadn't bothered to untie the knot from the bucket and as he weaved through the kitchen the threads of the rope snagged on the doorframe. Quickly, Joseph rotated his body around the bucket, a maneuver that prevented the water from spilling out, then flicked and pulled the rope to gain more slack before hurrying to the bedroom.

"Hold this," he said to John, as he thrust the bucket into his arms. "Don't let it go." The boy wrapped his arms around the cold, wet metal.

Agatha handed the baby to Joseph and he plunged it chest deep into the bucket. There was no wait. The baby cried and wriggled, madly.

"Thank God!" shouted Agatha, her body shuddered with excitement.

Pulling the baby from the water, Joseph snuggled him against his chest. "What beautiful dark eyes you have," he whispered to his newborn son. The boy appeared so terribly small and fragile in his thick, cold hands. After he wiped the blood from around the baby's mouth with his shirt sleeve, Joseph kissed the wet tuft of black hair on his head and handed him to Margaret, who'd undone the top of her dress to cradle the baby next to her bosom. The boy's small arms flung in opposite directions like some beautiful martyr.

Margaret looked up at Joseph and smiled. "You see. He'll be fine," she said, softly.

"And who would I be to doubt your angels?" He smiled back at her.

THE STORY UNDERNEATH

Beth Goobie

The free library on 14th Street is a glass-doored cabinet perched on a post,
its exterior painted with shelves and the red, blue, green spines of books.
No lock, no security guard; the rose-petaled knob was carved
for the grasp of a ten-year-old or a babe in arms.
Inside, a rainbow of books crams haphazardly,
novel atop memoir, Harry Potter nudging Alice Munro.
The woman who instigated this miscellany stands at her window
and watches an anticipation of readers approach alone or in family groups –
children running ahead and jumping up to see through the glass doors,
adults giving each other cautious smiles and two metres' sanctuary.
Ten minutes before noon, a semi pulls up and a man gets out.
He opens the cabinet doors, rummages in a frown of contemplation,
extracts two paperbacks and replaces them with the six in his bag.
As the semi rumbles off, the woman wonders if those two books
will take him out of Saskatchewan, east toward la belle province,
or south to the queen's city before the semi rumbles to a stop
beside another boulevard library, where the trucker will climb down
to exchange one chapter in his journey of story with the next.

It's been one month since the public libraries closed their doors
to virus and patrons alike and, city-wide, readers are scanning
cereal boxes and jam jar labels for possible plots and protagonists,
anything to invite story into soul. At the 14th Street free library,
the woman at her living room window has been observing
a now decade-long dialogue carried on between borrowers
who place small bits of themselves inside those glass doors –
a name written on the inside of a dog-eared cover, beside *Christmas 1995*,
pages decorated with chocolate fingerprints and coffee-stained musings
that anyone could do without. In this time when everyone is doing without,
humanity's lungs breathe in rhythm, calling in the merciful air
and wishing it deep into the lungs of the suffering,
trying to absorb some part of their struggle, lift it free.

This awareness underlies a day's choices like a story
surfacing into consciousness. Hour after hour, so many stories depart
untold – small lost words, each a last breath crossing the lips and gone.

Those left breathing sense the void in their own mouths,
and the blankness that drops down sometimes,
as if the synapses in healthy brains are also going out, one by one,
in sympathy with the greater pattern. But it is the smaller that,
synapse by synapse, creates the greater. The free library on 14th Street
is one node in a pattern, one mouth calling past its shock,
the X on a fantasy novel map that guides seekers toward heartbeat,
the story that continues. The woman at her living room window watches
civilization, bookended by two metres' hope for the future, come and go
on her boulevard – a civilization that goes on building bridges, driving semis,
standing behind cash registers, pulling on gowns, gloves and face masks
and facing down death so the living can dream road trips
and summer music festivals and babies and handshakes and hugs
and falling in love with all the stories yet to breathe us.

DINERS IN A DANGEROUS TIME

dee Hobsbawn-Smith

While I sauté onions with garlic and ginger for tonight's curry, Mom perches on the top of three steps that lead to the living room, her wineglass on the counter beside her, our dog Jake waiting hopefully at her knee as she eats a slice of my sourdough bread. Mom is here for supper; she's a widow, part of my husband's and my tripod-shaped bubble from the beginning of the pandemic. But Mom can't really smell the ginger in my pan. She suffers from anosmia; when she lost her sense of smell a few decades ago, not only did she lose the ability to distinguish smells, but she lost any interest she might have had in cooking. For years, everything she ate tasted like scorched nuts or burnt beans, and she could only distinguish the most pungent odours – garlic, caramelized sugar. That loss is bitterly ironic, given that anosmia is one of the markers of Covid-19. It can take months or longer for sufferers to regain the ability to smell, and with it, the facility for enjoying food. A friend of mine, Jenni Lessard, a chef, is suffering from anosmia as a result of Covid-19. Three months after she was diagnosed, her senses are maybe eighty-five per cent returned. Peanut butter remains an icky brown paste, and the fragrance of fresh jasmine blossoms eludes her, but she is plagued by weird phantom smells. For a chef, such a loss is critical, even in the short term; Jenni doesn't know when her sense of smell will return in its entirety, but she is acting on faith that it will.

I've been thinking about food a lot lately. I'm a chef like Jenni, but retired from the professional kitchen. However, I remain deeply involved with what and how we eat, as a writer and as a conscious, involved eater. I cook every day, and have for decades, so that remains a constant in my life, one that brings me comfort and calm. But I know of many who can't cook, and I worry more and more for their wellbeing. So while there's nothing new about the fact that I think about food every day, two reasons for extra attention have collided: the pandemic, of course; and second, the thesis I am writing for my Master's degree, a novella-length paper about two extraordinary food writers.

The pandemic has most of us thinking more about how we feed ourselves. There's all kinds of evidence of this – measure out countless images on social media of loaves of homemade sourdough bread, and empty shelves in markets where flour and yeast used to sit in abundant rows we all took for granted. Add lineups to gain access to grocery stores, online shopping, closed restaurants, lineups to get into the farmers' market, news about a coming spike in food prices, lineups to buy wine and beer. Stir in worry about the survival of family farms, worry over immigrant employees of slaughterhouses doing difficult work in confined and dangerous situations, and for migrant farmworkers' health and safety as they live and harvest our food in inhospitable conditions, worry for the wellbeing of frontline health workers, worry about the safety of truckers and the other threads of our fragile global food chain, about local farmers keeping their farms viable for another season, about hungry kids missing out on school lunch programs, about hungry, homeless, and disadvantaged people as food banks and soup kitchens close or slow down. Mix in our enduring undercurrents of worry about food-crop monocultures, the health of the land we all rely on, dying animals and ecosystems, climate change… the recipe is, as they say, fraught.

The stresses are monumental. Good cheer is in short supply. We are marked by our masks as we go about our days, but we are most marked by absence – the simple physical contact that humanity is all about. No hugs. No cooking together. No sitting at the same table. No sharing a meal. No coffee breaks, no wine socials, no teatime with buddies. We remain at the double-arms'-length dictated by the need for social distance, and are confined to quarters and family bubbles by lockdowns.

So of course we are thinking more about our food, backlit by fears of the effects a pandemic – and a former president to the south – might have on our ability to feed ourselves and our families. All of these make it hard to take true pleasure in our daily bread, but it matters that we do: we are nourished in other, intangible ways when we eat well, when we take pleasure in eating, when we set aside our metaphoric anosmia.

Beyond the pandemic, the university thesis I'm writing also has me thinking more about why food and writing about food matters, especially now. I'm writing about the century-apart dialogue between two epicurean writers – M.F.K. Fisher and Jean Anthelme Brillat-Savarin, a French lawyer born in 1755. Fisher, an American born in 1908, is an icon to many food lovers, author of more than twenty books, mostly written in the personal narrative style she pioneered that has since become the template of modern food writing. Her books include *With Bold Knife and Fork*, *Map of Another Town*, and *The Art of Eating*, an omnibus collection of five of her early books, among them *The Gastronomical Me* and *How to Cook A Wolf*. It's an odd but interesting fact that the latter, on survival cooking, was written during the Second World War, a time of global hardship due to rationing of staples in order to feed the troops. The wolf of the title is the wolf at the door, a reminder that hard times have come before, and that, as Fisher writes, to "nourish ourselves with all possible skill, delicacy and ever-increasing enjoyment," we "assert and then reassert our dignity in the face of poverty and war's fears and pains." Easy enough to substitute "pandemic" for "poverty and war," although they, too, loom in the shadow with our other fears.

Fisher translated Brillat-Savarin's book, the 1825 classic, *The Physiology of Taste*, in 1949. The chatty old food lover's text is still in print, and has become a culinary touchstone. It is an interesting combo of aphorisms for which he is still famous – among them "Tell me what you eat, and I will tell you who you are" and "The destiny of nations depends on how they nourish themselves" – coupled with anecdotes, musings on all manner of foods and subjects related (some only tangentially) to eating, and essays in the form of meditations. He was a provincial lawyer, a *bon vivant* and gastronome fond of hunting, music, pretty women, and food, and he lived through one of France's most difficult eras, the French Revolution, including the Reign of Terror, when Robespierre and his cronies set up guillotines around the country to lop off the heads of their political opponents, nobles, priests, and those suspected of hoarding food. But Brillat-Savarin – a conservative-minded Royalist – survived, and would bear witness in his book to the emergence of restaurants, created by out-of-work cooks and chefs whose employers, mostly the elite nobility, had died on the guillotine. Restaurants have since become a normal part of our lives until they suddenly weren't, when the economics of Covid-19 forced many to close and others to cut back. Brillat-Savarin's observations on the origins of restaurants form a small but insightful part of an engaging book, a book at times pedantic, entirely non-chronological, prone to riffs, flights of fancy, and linguistic puns, but engrossing despite its dated language. His curious 19th century brain considered the many ways in which food was implicated in his life, from medicine and science to hunting, travel, and his doings in the presence of beautiful women, especially his cousin, Juliette

Récamier. Plus there was that small detail of the Revolution, which he fled at risk for his life, forced into exile to Switzerland and later the United States, all recounted in remarkably calm anecdotes. His exile ended when the Revolution did, and he returned to France, but he lost his provincial home and lived out his days in Paris, where, when he self-published *The Physiology*, his friends were astounded to learn he was the author. He died a year after its publication. So history, death, and war were inextricably woven into the fabric of how Brillat-Savarin liked to eat and what he thought about that could possibly be viewed as being related to food.

Fisher's footnotes, annotations, and introduction to Brillat-Savarin's work bumped up the word count of the book in its 1949 edition by twenty per cent. But her interjections also added a new perspective – a working-class woman's, youthful, living and toiling in another century. She was becoming a famous writer and would be recognized by the literary world as one of the finest prose stylists of her generation, with an opinionated and educated palate, a taste for life in Europe, for good food and good drink. An early feminist, Fisher was determined to live by her own lights, and had two daughters, one out of wedlock by an unnamed lover, and three husbands – one of whom, the love of her life, died by suicide when faced with a terrible disease that was responsible for the amputation of one leg and would take the other plus his arms – unless. So he did the "unless," shooting himself in 1941 when the pain became unbearable. But a year earlier, he and Fisher briefly returned to Europe, where they had previously lived happily, to buy pain medications unavailable in the USA. On that trip, they saw on the ships and European trains the evidence of the Second World War – refugees, soldiers, prisoners, one of whom committed suicide in front of them to escape his captors. All of this Fisher recounts in *The Gastronomical Me*, in a moving meditation on loss and grief bracketed by other essays on how she learned to love and appreciate good food, alone and in company. Years after her husband's death, Fisher would live in Europe again with her young daughters, writing about places, flavours, and eating well as an integral part of life. She ended her years in a small house in a vineyard in northern California, where she was visited by her many admirers and friends.

Fisher and Brillat-Savarin both survived wars and great personal losses. Their writing about food reflected their lives, as good writing – and other art forms – often does. In both cases, their words were charged with humour, empathy, compassion, wit, even as they wrote about death, loss, exile, grief. Those intangibles combined with their wine, their French cheeses, their *pâtés* and oysters and artichokes and *haricots verts* in season, all the intangibles of a life lived fully adding some other intensified, ephemeral, and unquantifiable level of meaning and flavour to their meals, their appetites, their lives.

We too need that other level of meaning. Our lives are equally fraught, in these Covid times. Our list of worries and risks and grief grows globally as the numbers of illnesses and deaths climb. Hope, that elusive bird with feathers, might seem impossible, or inconsequential, or unlikely to help. But hope is the seasoning that we need to get past any metaphoric sense of anosmia we suffer from. We still need to eat. And sharing still helps. Fisher and Brillat-Savarin both knew this as truth.

So with our plates of hand-cranked pasta and loaves of homemade sourdough bread, with our bowls of pinto beans, our beef stew and our vegan burgers, with our local artisan beer and our ethically-sourced coffee, surely we can find within ourselves the compassion, the generosity, the kindness, the good grace, the love, and hope to feed our loved ones, our neighbourhood kids, our elders, ourselves, our immigrants. Surely we can create home-cooked food seasoned with all those intangibles to sustain us. The equation is so simple: home-cooked + share = hope.

LET'S DO THIS AGAIN

Chelsea Coupal

Hope you're staying safe and healthy. Are you guys OK?
We're doing OK, doing fine. These are weird times.
Swallow and smile hard on Zoom calls.
You're on mute, they say. You're on mute. You're muted.

Text friends too often or not at all. Virtual Friday drinks and say:
I feel like I'm in your living room. Are you guys OK? *We're doing OK,*
doing fine. These are weird times. Let's do this again.
(And then never do.) Shop for a mask. Shop wearing a mask,

disinfect the grocery basket. Shop six feet apart. Touch and tug at
the mask, and touch it again. Squint eyes to show I'm smiling
hard behind it. Smile, turn off the webcam, mic on mute,
read another poem that captures the mood.

Shop wearing a mask. Disinfect the shopping cart. Are you guys OK?
You're on mute, they say. Hope you're staying safe and healthy.
These are weird times. Touch and tug at the mask. *We're doing OK,*
doing fine. Swallow our hearts. We're all living six feet apart.

THE YEAR I THOUGHT I'D GET MARRIED

Chelsea Coupal

I touch my grandmother's face through glass.
I don't stand outside and sing, but I see people on TV do it.
Flock of flesh, no feathers or wings; just pianos,
saxophones, hands clapping. The infection is visible

and invisible. The days are flies crowding
an open wound, days-old, exposed; a knee skinned
deep in the woods, a gash on a doe's back. I wish I was single
and in high school, so I could kiss my date through glass

patio doors – press my palms against them, undress myself
with unsteady fingers, marvel at the body
on just the other side. These days are only slow
and lonely. I can't see the ocean from here and wonder

if I will again. But everything moves in waves –
wild grass shimmers on prairie hills in August wind,
snow snakes across gravel roads in winter, pickerel swim
in sync, their scales slick-silver and flickering-green.

FIDELITY

Allison Kydd

Veronica sits at the bay window in the living-room most mornings, sits until guilt (or sheer boredom) sends her off to accomplish some small task. Oh, yes, she's keeping a list: get dressed, brush hair, make bed, put away clothes, balance bank statement, water plants, try new recipe, sweep or vacuum, phone X, Y or Z, finish letter to M, practise standing warrior, shoulder rolls, downward facing dog…. Not that she ever makes it to the end of the list, but she scribbles it out anyway.

Otherwise, she might not bother getting out of bed. He has little to say about it, though she knows he worries. Once or twice he's asked if she's depressed, if that's why she's sleeping so much.

"Everyone is depressed," she says. "It's the state of the world. How can anyone not be depressed?"

She knows she's overreacting, but she resents the question when obviously she's not the kind to give in, no matter what she's up against. She's always been able to lick her wounds and then get on with things.

Or so she tells herself.

And how dare he anyway? He used to compliment her willingness to fight any battle. Like when she was being hooked up to that intravenous bag once a week. He'd watch as the needle went into her arm, would sit beside her, read to her for hours while the poison did its work. Almost twenty years ago now. Not that much drama in their lives anymore, especially not for the last year.

He mustn't give up on her now. After all, she isn't lying when she says she's committed to him, and being committed means one can't afford to fail. Though it's okay for her to have doubts now and then—she knows she doesn't mean anything by them—he mustn't ever think he made another mistake. Nor can she let him know how dependent she really is. Not that he would leave her high and dry.

Actually, he's not perfect either. He's one to be annoyed by small things: lights left on, music too loud, blinds left open at night. (People might see them from the street—as if anyone cared!) Fortunately, such fussiness is a small sin. She doesn't want to imagine how distant he could be if he didn't love her anymore. The thought gives her an ache in her belly.

She once had a run of other lovers, not that it matters. For almost twenty years, she's seldom thought of them. If they've come to mind more frequently of late, it's because she has so much time on her hands. This wasn't a good year to quit her job, though she didn't feel she'd had a choice—when the desire was gone and she seldom even liked her students. Unfortunately, when she decided to retire, she had no way of predicting that the world would change within a few months.

When thoughts of former lovers do come to mind, there's little sweetness in the memories, certainly not when she thinks of Kurt, though there must have been something in the beginning. She's not a total masochist.

It's hard to believe she tolerated the things Kurt did and said. Oh, no, he wasn't abusive, not really, but he wasn't kind either. He simply refused to take her feelings into account if doing so would cramp his style. It sometimes seemed that he set out to humiliate her.

She remembers one Sunday afternoon when a group of them were having lunch at a friend's. They had ordered pizzas. Kurt, as always, was the centre of attention. Before long, he was flirting with one of the other women, then followed the woman into the basement. Time went by, but neither emerged. Veronica tried to pretend she wasn't going out of her mind, while no one else seemed to think it peculiar. Was it possible he would bed another woman in the middle of the day while she—supposedly his girlfriend, his partner—was practically within earshot? This was a new level of cruelty. Or was it some kind of ploy to get rid of her? He had always been frank about not wanting a permanent relationship.

She counted the minutes. Ten minutes, twenty. What could they be doing? Why was it taking so long? What was she supposed to do?

She stood up, collected her coat and purse and headed for the kitchen door. This was noticed.

"What's happening?"

"I think she's leaving."

"What's up? Shouldn't you tell Kurt?" That was Sean, the fellow who had driven them to the gathering. At least he was speaking directly to her rather than about her. The expression on his face—what was it? Pity? Discomfort? Incredulity? She didn't know.

"You tell him," she blurted out. "He's your friend."

She couldn't say anymore. The tears were threatening to flow.

Sean had followed her to the kitchen.

"Look, Ronnie," he said. "You've got to toughen up. Things aren't always as bad as they might seem."

She shoved her feet into her boots and looked past him towards the living-room.

"Thanks for the pizza and coffee," she hollered to the others, then bolted out into the cold.

It wasn't the first time she'd stumbled down a sidewalk when blinded by tears, but Kurt had never been quite so blatant. It wasn't long before they caught up to her in the car. Sean was driving, of course, and Kurt scrunched up against Sean's girlfriend in the front seat. The third couple were in the back, but not looking at her, thank heavens. Probably too embarrassed. How had this suddenly become her fault?

The car slowed. She slowed. The car stopped, she stopped.

"Get in," Kurt hissed from the car window, not opening the door.

What right had he to be angry?

She stayed where she was, not crying anymore, but with tracks of tears frozen on her cheeks. He got out finally and came over to her. She noticed he didn't have a coat.

"What are you trying to prove?" he said.

"What am I trying to prove? What about you?"

"Listen. It's bloody cold out here. Get in the car."

She turned and headed in the opposite direction.

Kurt went back to the car, exchanged a few words with Sean, and then the car pulled away. When Kurt caught up to her, he was struggling to stuff his arms into Sean's winter coat.

"C'mon," he said, "you're an idiot. I'll walk you home."

By the time they reached her place, they were both thoroughly chilled, and he had persuaded her that he wasn't answerable to her for his behaviour. She could choose to trust him or not. She chose to accept his rationale, not that he ever explained what he had been doing in the basement, though it was possible he was helping the woman with an assignment or even smoking a joint with her.

Nor was that the only time Kurt courted another woman before her eyes. No need, in fact, for him to remove their clothes, since he could make love with lingering glances, witty comments, the slightest touch. He knew the effect he had and how to make a woman fall for him.

Ronnie knew this as well because he constantly worked his magic on her. Even now, thirty-five years later, she doesn't entirely trust herself, would never take the risk of seeing him again. Fortunately, he lives far away, so there isn't really any danger.

Not that she doesn't fantasize about it and set up the scene, careful to give herself the upper hand.

In her fantasies, she's always gorgeous. After all, she runs regularly and doesn't skip her yoga practice. She's even joined a gym (or had before the pandemic), so she doesn't look her age or suffer the aches and pains of arthritis. After all, it's important that Kurt would want her, in order to give some spice to her rejection.

*

She knows it would be easy to find him, since she knows the city where he lives, knows which university. Finding him would be no more difficult than making the trip and finding a space in the visitors' parking lot. No doubt his name is in the directory, along with his department and office number. She could take the elevator up to Fourth Floor: Humanities, figure out how the numbering works.

Before making her way down the appropriate hallway, she would need to find the "Ladies" room. With any luck it wouldn't be one of those places where everything is co-ed. Imagine encountering him as he's just zipping up after having a pee, sharing the same wash basin, as they used to do when tidying up after sex. What a laugh that would be. His look of consternation seeing her like this, and yet, and yet…. He would probably handle it with the same poise that he handles every other intimate encounter. No, meeting him in his office would definitely be wiser.

She looks in the mirror. Wonders what he would see. Hair gone grey, longer and thicker because she can't go to the salon during the lockdown. But that would be okay; he always liked her a bit untidy. Eyeliner? Pull off her mask and freshen her lipstick? But that would be too obvious. Besides, she can still get away with little or no makeup. After all these years.

What if he wasn't in his office? Just for a second she would falter. After all, she doesn't know his teaching schedule. He might be with a student. Ha! She can imagine what kind of session, especially if the student were young and female. But that's not fair; he's always been an original, would never fall into that cliché.

There would be another pause at his office door. Perhaps it's ajar, suggesting he's inside or close by. No doubt she would be breathless. Heart pounding, would suddenly know it was a very bad idea.

At that point, she would begin to walk away without knocking.

*

And that's the truth of it! Even in her imagination she can't get the upper hand. How ridiculous to imagine she could ever make him suffer.

After Kurt came Sean, yes the same Sean, but not for long, and then Daniel. Daniel, of course, was quite a different story. If only he hadn't made it too easy for her by caring too much. Because she was suddenly the one with the power to betray, betray him she did. She's ashamed of it now, of course, knows it was her fault. So, it seemed she had lost them both—Kurt who kept her on tenterhooks and possibly never loved her, and Daniel, who made her face the frightening reality of being needed.

When both were gone, she thought for a time she would never love or be loved again, that in fact she didn't deserve it. Not that it stopped her from looking. There were lots of possibilities before, between and after Kurt and Daniel, and she too learned the art of the convenient exit. Sometimes she has difficulty remembering all the names.

Until the rules changed and she found she wasn't immortal.

She remembers the gynecologist, an East Indian woman, trim and dark, with slightly greying hair coiled smoothly into a French knot. Crisp white coat over long navy pants. The tag on her pocket said Dr. Zarah Hamal, the name as elegant and competent as the woman herself.

She wanted Dr. Hamal to like her, so she tried to smile bravely, but she was cold and uncomfortable there on the table and embarrassed by the bleeding that wouldn't stop. One of Dr. Hamal's slender gloved hands was on her belly as the other explored Ronnie's intimate parts. Some gasps, pressure and minor pains later, the doctor invited her to get dressed and then whisked away.

Sore and awkward, Ronnie had barely made herself decent when she heard the polite knock on the door of the examination room.

"Come in," she said, finally managing to fasten her slacks and wriggle into her pullover. She had folded down the soiled sheet so they wouldn't have to look at the mess, but she saw the doctor glance there anyway.

The doctor took a seat by the table.

"I think you know it's not good news," she said.

Ronnie nodded. What else could she do? Was she imagining a miracle?

"There's a significant growth, but I've scheduled an MRI, just to be sure."

"Of course. Thank you."

"Have you any questions?"

"I don't think so. Will you...? Will I see you again?"

Why had she asked that? Was she so afraid of being alone? There was a pause before the reply.

"You'll go to the hospital for the procedure. The receptionist will give you the particulars when you leave."

"Thank you." Again, she tried to smile but couldn't quite manage.

*

Considering everything, she had no right to call Daniel after the cancer diagnosis, but she needed someone and could think of no-one else. Fortunately, because they had run into each other a few times over the years, she knew how to reach him.

Neither was there any earthly reason for him to respond. But he came less than an hour after she'd sent her message, wrapped his arms around her and wept. She supposed it was for all the wasted time and tried not to think too much about it.

Later that night, in her bed, she could tell that he too was lying awake.

"I can't believe this," he said. "Why now?"

She thought she understood.

"We'll beat this," he said.

"We'll." She wasn't about that. After all, it was her body, her cancer.

*

Now, he has come downstairs. Ronnie hears him filling the coffee pot with water, grinding just enough beans for one, putting them in the filter, closing the lid, plugging in the coffee maker and clicking the switch.

They quarreled this morning, some little irritation she scarcely remembers, but she does remember snapping at him. He can be so touchy sometimes.

For the most part, however, they've had a good life together. She'll always be grateful she wasn't alone during the chemo sessions, and so far she's been lucky, almost twenty years and there's been no recurrence. Other than that, she tries not to admit how much need is there, focuses on the fact they're good companions and try to be considerate.

Her brush with mortality has made both of them cautious as well, more cautious than she would like to be. So what if they are the poster couple for Covid precautions—never go anywhere, never see anyone unless masked and distanced and almost sanitized to death!

Now she remembers. That was where the quarrel started. She wanted to go to a restaurant for supper, just the two of them, since restrictions had just been lifted in their part of the province.

He was reluctant, and she exploded. "There's still a world out there," she said, "we can't hide here for ever."

"You're prepared to risk it?" he asked. "Don't you know you're in a high-risk category?"

"That was twenty years ago," she said.

"I know when it was," he said.

"I think you're using it as an excuse," she said, suddenly indignant. "I think you like the way things are. It gives you a way to keep me all to yourself."

She could tell from his face that he was hurt and angry, but couldn't seem to stop.

"I think you need to set me free," she said. What the fuck did she mean by that?

"That," he said, "is about the stupidest thing I've ever heard. Did you learn that from one of your old boyfriends?"

A bit too close to the mark there, she thought.

"Have it your own way," she said and thumped upstairs.

So there went the morning. They made separate lunches and ate them separately as well. She checked off a few items, went outside and filled the birdfeeder, which wasn't even on the list. But all the time, she knew she had overstepped the boundary that protected them from being too real, and she would have to make it up.

"Daniel," she calls, "come and sit."

At first he doesn't respond, and she's not surprised, doesn't blame him. She calls him again.

His voice is tense.

"Do you really feel you're trapped? Do you really want to get away from me?"

"Oh, Danny," she says, "must you take everything so seriously? I'm just tired of it all, being so limited. (She must be very careful here.) I'm sorry I took it out on you."

He's silent, so she waits. After a minute, she says it again,

"Come and sit. Please, my love."

The bay window is still her favourite place from which to view the world. She looks out over the front lawn, the flower gardens and the picket fence that borders the street, where sometimes she sees neighbours walking by, especially if the blinds are wide open. There are birds at the feeder and, in spring, an apple tree in bloom.

In spite of what he must still be feeling, he pulls out a chair, just as she hoped he would. She's giddy with relief, knowing he's about to forgive her again. As he lowers himself to sit, she smiles, wills him to reach out and stroke her hair, knows she really should stop testing him this way.

When they were younger, even ten years ago, this moment would have been consummated in bed, coffee burning dry or not. It was how they protected themselves from feeling too much. But these days, they're a little less fragile. Water under the bridge isn't always a bad thing. When they make love now, they're tender rather than desperate, and it's often enough to sit side by side, gazing out the same window on the world.

A NEW WORLD, A BLAZING WORLD
For Agni

Carla Barkman

What god shall we adore with our oblations?

He had that last beer, the third chocolate-chip cookie. Now Agni dismembered, his bones become pines, his muscles coarse grass, blood and bile the minerals we mix with greens to steel ourselves against the many hours. To become silver. Every morning examine the Twitter feed, every evening Instagram, each octothorpe a shield in eight directions. And yet there is a breach. Flummoxed. Moss on the rocks, snakes and nectarines, peddling coconut oil, bootlegging hydroxychloroquine, nebules of bleach.

What now shall we abhor with our oblations?

Morphine, rocuronium, body bags in short supply and all the chains exhausted. Shrouds are too airy, we are told, and don't dislodge the tubes, a spiky package. To the morgue within the hour. Mothers mouth farewells from glassed-in rooms. We don garbage bags instead of gowns, run protected code blues. Hot and cold zones morph and spill. The neck is a vulnerable area, as are the wrists, too bare. Carbon dioxide exhaled and inhaled, THC to combat lethargy, rum and mushrooms for despair. Until we are high on it. Until we are settled.

What is beautiful?

My mother's disappointment, grey silk on a hanger, grey linen. She pictured herself at sea. Kittens paw each other by the wood stove, sesame and bergamot, ginger and turmeric concoction. We thought we might assemble après-ski over frog leg and alligator fondue. Kitchari now to balance the doshas, watermelon curry, eggplant stew. Italian apartment block becomes a columbarium, Dolce & Gabanna scarves at half mast, Juliet on the balcony forever. Canals clear in Venice, goats at a Welsh McDonald's, deer and wild horses. Chocolate lab leaps between pines, his head full of pheasants.

What happiness?

My sister hides vinegar in Sprite bottles to make us spin and spin we do, peristeronic. Cooing and cawing. Rub cream into each other's psoriatic scalps, rummy and whist, rice crackers and cheese before dinner. The best possible words, the precise words: not *do not attempt to resuscitate* but *allow natural death to occur.* Futile, when lungs are consumed, made plastic. Dovecotes crumble in the Cotswolds, ruinous abbeys, roofs incessantly leaking. Let the tumbling fall. We destroy what we love when we love it too well. She is scolded. We are made to sit in the corner, eyes streaming.

The world's a-blazing. Agni in the smoke, gone back to the heavens.

ESSENTIAL WORK

Madonna Hamel

I pulled up to the house just as the *shelter-in-place* order came through. Before unpacking the car, I explored every room, clapping my hands with glee. "I'm here!" I hooted. I'm *actually* writer-in-residence in Wallace Stegner's childhood home.

I pulled my journal from my knapsack and planned to get down to work over a steak at the hundred-year-old Jack's Café. But Jack's was *closed due to Covid*. Highway 13, the main thoroughfare, otherwise known as Red Coat Trail, was empty, except for a fellow sitting on a bench across the street. He waved and hollered across to me.

"How ya doin?"

"I'm great," I hollered back. "Considering."

"Considering what?" he asked.

Despite the sunny, warm spring day, no one walked the banks of the Frenchman River. No children played in the schoolyard up the street. No squealing. No running. No skipping. Maybe girls don't skip anymore. They probably don't dance in a circle, either, holding hands and singing that Black Death ditty....

Ring around the rosie,
Pocket full of posie,
Husha husha,
We all fall down...

oblivious to the fact that the *rosie ring*, a blotch on the skin, was the first sign of plague. And the *pocket of posie* referred to small bouquets of flowers and herbs you stuffed in your pockets to ward away death. *Husha*, was originally *achoo*, the final sound a body made as it succumbed.

*

On the ides of March, just before driving to Eastend, my friend Page and I made a video.

"We interrupt this surveillance," I hollered over the wind into his camera, "with this newsflash. Deep sources confirm the latest correspondence from the planet – this planet Earth – is indeed authentic. Issued this morning

– not digitally, but by hand, in cursive – the Earth claims to have come to the end of her patience with her tenants – those not behaving as stewards – and realizes they simply can't – or won't – stop clobbering the animals, clotting the waters or clouding her skies.

"So, mom Earth has decided to take matters back into her own calloused and ever-loving hands. The God of Dirt has spoken. And she's sending us to our rooms. *Just go home*, she says. *Sit down. Take some deep, deep breaths. Count to a hundred. And think. About. What. You've. Done.*

"She strongly advises that, for the duration, there be no buying no selling no squandering no pushing no shoving no bullying no threatening no exceeding our grasping no marketing no stealing no consuming no billion users using no golden rings. No dressing for success in the name of progress. No need to impress. No full-court press. No heedlessly hurrying to fill our soul-shaped holes.

"Consider yourself served. In fact, she says, *I've been serving you all along. And now it's time for a collective dose of tough love, so, consider yourself grounded.*

"Your mom,

"Planet Earth.

"P.S. Just to cheer you up, she says, I've restocked the canals of Venice with little fishes. Actually, you did, just by NOT doing anything. By backing off. By *going home*. It's worth noting that some countries are already moving the homeless into hotels. Because, in order to go home, you have to have a home to go to."

*

The year I graduated from art school I got a job at a Vancouver gallery, teaching street kids the art of performance. *Ha. Me* teach *them.* They spent their days on sidewalks performing, pitching for spare change. But they talked fast, not used to having more than four seconds to get their story across. I had to get them to slow down, expand their repertoire. They spoke in terse haikus, but held long, full stories, too. By the age of eighteen, most of them looked world-weary, like they held too much.

"We're giving you a night on stage." I reminded them. "People are coming to hear you. *Paying* to hear you. So, speak sloooowllllly." I shared the old broadcasting rule of thumb: when it starts to sound too slow, that's when it's just right.

On performance night, they were crackling with energy.

"OK," I said to them backstage. "Just remember: People are sitting in chairs. They are not going anywhere. So, milk it."

And they did. But one eighteen-year-old named Juniper stands out. Her words worked their way into my thoughts, like a permanent sliver, resurfacing every time I marvel at the ways shameless greed gets framed as *genius*.

"Do morals even matter when fortune takes over?" she asked.

Standing in her long black raincoat and her straight black hair, she slayed us. She humbled us. And then, along with the others, she slipped back into the street.

*

My initial excitement about being in Stegner's childhood home wears off by the start of my fourth week. It gets replaced by an antsy, edgy, darkness I interpret as a desire to surround myself with my own stuff. I need my soul essentials, my books, my photographs, my little ritual objects – smudge sticks, votive candles, Mary statues and animal bones. I need my plants that I rarely water and my guitar that I never play. I need my own home.

On my birthday my old school chum toasts me on this new thing called *Zoom*. She and hubby are in their Toronto dining room. At one point, they step away from the screen to join a collective 7:30 p.m. cheer for *essential service personnel*. Off screen, while I sit staring at a potted plant in an empty room, people bang pots and dogs bark.

"Are you doing this where you are?" My friend asks when she returns. "It feels great!"

"In a town of, like, thirteen?" I say. "The geese are louder. So, how are you coping?"

"Oh, I'm fine. I'm still working. Movies have been declared *an essential service*."

"No kidding."

"I know," she says. "It's stupid."

*

In April, I'm staying up late, doom-scrolling on my computer. I get hooked on late night talk shows. Initially, it's fascinating to watch celebrity guests at home with their kids and their spouses and their bookshelves. Lost without studio lights, fanfare and audience applause, they ease off on their show-biz schtick. In fact, they seem to forget they're talking to millions of us, not just Jimmy, and whine about deprivations and inconveniences, redefine for the rest of us the meaning of *essential*. They are stuck in their houses (*no, not our L.A. place, our London place*) they complain. They have to exercise in the basement, cook, vacuum, do laundry. They even have to dye their own hair. From a box.

At the end of the show, having saved so much by slumming it, they give extravagantly to their favourite charity. But rest assured, the next day, come lunch time, they won't be hunting around in the back of the fridge for that half-jar of peanut butter because of last night's generosity.

I understand, it's not the fault of the rich and famous that 550,000 Americans are homeless. It's not even their responsibility. But it's moments like these when the great Western chasm, the yawning trench between *haves* and *have nots*, is fully revealed.

The kings and queens of media, be they leftie actors, or right-wing talk show hosts, or the op-ed anchors of misnamed *news programs*, comprise the *de facto* ruling class, writes George Saunders in his essay *The Braindead Megaphone*.

"The Conservative Opinion King," he goes on to write, " has more in common with the Liberal Opinion King than either does with the liberal and conservative slaughterhouse workers in Wichita; the Opinion Kings have friends in common, similar ambitions, a common frame of reference (agents, expected perks, a knowledge of the hierarchy of success indicators, a mastery of insider jargon)."

Add to that: wardrobe, make-up, drivers, dressers, make-up artists, and, of course, stylists to dye their hair.

*

For eleven years I worked at a radio station in Quebec City's old town. One week, in 2000, I kept pitching the same story every day. The roof of St. Roch mall, in the city's first working class district, was about to be removed. The idea was to revive some of the *ancien quartier*'s charm by exposing the old shops and paving stones. At the heart of it all stands St. Roch church, the size of a cathedral and built in the early 1600s. By removing the mall roof, the full glory of the church would be revealed, we were told.

"We should find out what's going to happen to the homeless who use the mall as a shelter when it's forty below," I suggested.

"The homeless aren't our listening audience," I was told.

"No shit," I grumbled. "What with them not having homes and all."

I kept trying. I wondered aloud what would happen to the man in the wheelchair with the mangled leg, and the other guy, with one arm and no teeth. And the kid with the emaciated dog. Eyes rolled. Here she goes again.

In the end, we did a number of stories on economic stimulus for green spaces, tourists and boutique hotels. We covered every angle of the story for *our listening audience.*

It's interesting to note that St. Roch, born in Montpelier in the Middle Ages, was a Franciscan monk who ministered to the sick and poor during the Black Death. It is said that anyone he prayed over was cured. Eventually, he succumbed to the plague himself. But before dying, he was rescued by a dog who found him languishing in the woods, his leg half-gone due to a festering wound. Today he is considered the patron saint against cholera, plague, skin rashes, contagious diseases, dogs and invalids with bad legs.

*

The Greek physician Socrates, in 400 BC, observed that people absorb topographical influences from the moment of birth, and that separation from such geographies could prove perilous. "These perturbations we now know as nostalgia and homesickness," writes Ronald Rees in *New and Naked Land.*

Rees was writing about immigrants and refugees coming to Canada to make a fresh start. People were so tied to certain landscapes they would give up good land for poorer land because it reminded them of home. "One of the strangest land-seeking phenomena," he writes, quoting a horseman living on the open prairie, "was the way in which experienced farmers, after trailing over innumerable townships in which there was nothing to offend the plough, would choose some stony lot, which, compared to what they might have had, was too poor to raise a disturbance."

Homesickness was a serious condition with often fatal results.

The Canadian government counted on a fatal homesickness when it removed indigenous people from their land – their Mother. When the Queen Mother, thousands of miles away, claimed ownership of prairie land, calling it "Crown title," she failed to understand there already existed an "underlying" title. "Raven title, Turtle title, Coyote title" have always been and continue to be home rule. Indigenous people never bought the story, writes L. Edward Chamberlain. His 2003 book is titled after the words of a Tsimshian elder asking government officials: *If this is your land, then where are your stories?*

Although nothing could be more out in the open than a body sleeping on a sidewalk, human homelessness, like human removal, is a story we don't like to tell. To tell ourselves the story of people with nowhere to go, is to tell *on* ourselves.

Empires have taught us the best way to erase a culture is to remove people from their land, ban their language, separate them from each other, demolish sacred sites and practices. So, it would follow the best way to revive a culture is to walk the land, behold the holy in each other and all creatures, and speak the language.

My last evening at Stegner, April 30, I step out at sunset, roaming for hours behind the nearby dinosaur museum, where a facsimile of T-Rex's bones reside. The weather is warm, Spring seems to be staying. I decide it's time to leave the attic of my brain and hold a wake for my *own* bones. I rub sage through my fingers, inhale deeply, and let the revivification begin. I leave some tobacco. I send a prayer to the evening darkness closing in, then start the long walk back to Wally's home.

Despite a nostalgia for his "place of snugness," his "little womb-village" on the "lovely-lonely exposed prairie," wrote Stegner in the essay *Child of the Far Frontier*, he learned to be at home wherever he was. "Having blown tumbleweed fashion around the continent," he grew to believe that home is not what you leave behind. "Home is what you can take away with you."

One out of 588 people in America are homeless. Before we get smug, we aren't doing much better up here. An estimated 235,000 people take shelter in Canada every year. Another friend in Toronto tells me she and her neighbours have converted their front yard libraries – outdoor cupboards of free books – to outdoor pantries. They are working together to get a vacant lot turned into a tent city. But they aren't getting a lot of support because, she says, people complain that "homeless people are dealing with addictions and nobody wants them around."

According to *homelesshub.ca*, 36 per cent of Canadians have been homeless or know someone who has been. Another 16 per cent fear they're next. One in seven humans without a home are children. If you live on a fixed income, experience a decline in health, and a raise in rent, if you have a disability or are a member of a visible minority or a refugee or an immigrant, if you're a kid kicked out of his house or a woman dodging a blow, or you're one paycheque away from the street and suddenly your boss loses his business due to a pandemic, you too could be homeless. You too, could be someone *nobody wants around them*.

In January 2021, *TIME* magazine revealed its "cover person of the year," newly elected Joe Biden and Kamala Harris.

Really? Not essential workers, anonymously modeling integrity and dignity, while the lucky among us fall apart in the safety of our homes, worrying our *blankees* and rationing toilet paper?

Or how about the least of our brothers and sisters, lacking essentials, stuck without a home?

But who am I to judge? I have heat, food and enough money squirreled away to get me through to spring. Back home in Val Marie after my stay in East End, for most of the year of the pandemic, I stay inside, venturing out only Tuesdays when the library and the Whitemud Grocery get their respective deliveries of books and chickens.

In his essay "Fiction to Make Sense of Life," Stegner observes that writers "are not creating machines that are going to do nothing but run… Fiction is more than a well-carpeted entertainment…more than a mirror… It's a lens." A lens he chose to focus on life in front of him, and chose to try and "make sense of it."

It's the post-modern fascination with the fun-house mirror of spectacle that sucks me into late night talk shows, despite my deep suspicion of bread-and-circuses diversions. I suspect, while glued to my screen, an essential worker or a homeless soul is succumbing to the moods and weather of the harsh world. Safe and sound in my home at a time when *the essentials* feel like luxuries, I am fortunate. And so, the least I can do is pull myself back to the task at hand and train my writer's lens on the essence of the situation. Before I pick up my pen and get back to work, I clap my hands to remind myself, *I'm still here.*

NO CONTACT DELIVERY

Delane Just

I order delivery from
2 blocks down the street,
collect McDonald's sticker vouchers

Buy 7 drinks, get one free.
Wash my money down with
an americano—2 cream.

Google recites
my credit card back to me.
I create furniture out of boxes,

Jenga in the corner, masks
by the door, ready
and waiting to exchange

Christmas presents
in January, at
6-feet, glasses fogged,
shouted pleasantries.

I RAN AND RAN BUT THE MICROSCOPIC WRECKING BALLS WITH SPIKES FLEW FAST ON MY HEELS

Jeanette Lynes

We dream in overdrive says the news.
The only way to not stay home at home is sleep.
Sleep is the new Wild West. As if the *old*
Wild West wasn't enough to bring us down.
A leash of deer lassoed me last night,
Their antlers jabbed, the main buck wracked
His brain against bark. I headed for the hills.
The mall. I'd always felt safe there in real life,
Foolish as that sounds. Its wall dissolved,
Opened into a deep, cold lake.
I once picnicked on its shore. My ex
Emerged where the mall's fourth wall used
To be. 'Oh believe *me*', I told him, 'I'll stay
Six feet from you. Six feet and four provinces'.
Then a fairy twittered by, she seemed nice enough.
Bid me make a wish. 'What is it you most
Want? Celery? Summer? A haircut? Or Love'?
But she flitted away on a cancelled flight.
The headless statue said I must change
My life. How I envied him, no head,
No need for a mask. I don't like advice
From headless dudes so I made a break
For autumn's crimson blaze and ache, a trail.
People with heads passed me, breathed
Their haloed fuzzball breaths. Their spores
Trying to smoke me but it was pretty, out there
In the flailing fall. Pretty as hell.

Morning: an antler shard.
Fluff of lint.
My jogging shoes readied by the bed.

PURIFICATION

CC *Corbett*

Grady's cold knuckles rapped against the cabin door. No one answered so he knocked again. A small voice called out from inside: "Spanish flu, go away."

"It's okay. I've had it."

"The doctor said no visitors."

"It's me, Charles Grady." Grady removed his service cap thinking the girl might recognize him without it and stepped in front of the window in case she could see him through the condensation. He hoped he wouldn't have to add the words "your stepfather." He straightened the tie of his soldier's uniform now permanently crumpled from the long train ride west. The uniform had helped him hitch a ride to the cabin from a local anxious to hear some war yarns and feed his need to be gracious to those who'd served.

The door creaked open on rusted hinges and Grady stepped inside carrying the same small pack and fiddle case he'd left with to go overseas four years earlier. He smoothed back his hair, suddenly conscious of how much greyer it looked. The room seemed empty at first but then he detected Ada shielded behind the front door. The roundness of her face had waned and she had grown a bit taller than Grady but she was not quite a young woman yet. Without speaking she led him to the back bedroom, covering her face with a gauze mask before she entered so that only her serious eyes were visible. Grady followed.

"Sam, it's me, Grady."

The colour drained from Grady's face as he saw Sam lying in bed, sweat beaded on his blistered forehead. Sam's head lolled from side to side as he attempted to open his eyes to see his visitor. They lit up for a second with what might have been recognition. Sam had taken him in after fire destroyed Grady's store and gave him a job driving the milk wagon. In return, Grady married Sam's young daughter when she contracted a case of fatherless conception.

"Troll," Sam mumbled. Blood trickled from his nostrils and Grady wiped it with his handkerchief. "Sorry...troll...doctor."

"Do you want some water?" Grady asked, setting down his cap to pick up a cup from the small table beside Sam's bed. Sam's hand waved through the air trying to push the cup away.

"Book…" Grady's eyes followed Sam's to the bedside table. On it lay a small maroon book. As Grady reached for it, Sam's eyes grew round.

"Wrong…hurt everybody," Sam managed. He gripped Grady's forearm. "Ada's father." Tears welled in Sam's eyes. His blue lips parted as he began to cough and the sheets caught a fine, red spray. From all of his time on the frontlines, Grady knew that when death was imminent, the best thing – the only thing – to do was to keep the victims calm, to try to give them peace during their final moments.

"Everything is okay." Grady patted Sam's hand.

Sam struggled to lift his head off the pillow. "Ada's father," he said. "Book."

"Do you want me to read this book?" Grady picked it up by its soft cover. Sam's fingers tightened around Grady's arm. He coughed again and blood shot out, his eyes and mouth opening wide. He couldn't breathe. His arms flailed through the air as he gasped.

"Sam!" Grady tried to sit him up. Sam's hand was locked onto Grady's forearm like a vice. Sucking sounded from Sam's throat as he choked on mucous. Grady pounded on Sam's back and when that didn't work, he lowered Sam down to rest against the pillow, rolling him onto his side. The pressure from Sam's hand slowly released. His lifeless stare fixated on the book. "Rest my friend," Grady whispered closing Sam's eyes. Grady turned to Ada. "Where is your mother?"

"In the yard," Ada said staring through the window, now wet with spring's tears.

"I didn't see her when I came in."

"We buried her last week."

Grady gulped as his fingers grasped the book. "Do you want to sit with your grandfather for a while and say goodbye?" he asked when he managed to catch his breath. As Grady stepped away from the bed, Ada approached to sit by Sam and hold his hand.

Grady walked into the next room and sat at the table pushing away dirty dishes and crumbs so he could read. *The little man played the fiddle again for us tonight. He is a lively entertainer but he is so short. I wish he would quit smiling at me.* He flipped through the pages recognizing his dead wife's loopy script until the book settled open on a dog-eared page. The pretty little letters in their pretty little lines told the tale of how Sophia had always been in love with someone else even from the start. Sweat bled into Grady's undershirt as he read what Sophia had been up to the night he and Sam were locked in the town jail for getting mixed up in a street brawl. While they were being attacked by drunk lumberjacks and then the police, the town doctor had ridden out to the cabin to make sure that Sophia was okay. The shame of finally learning that the doctor was Ada's father burned Grady's cheeks. His eye caught a word. *Troll.* That was the word Sam sputtered when he saw Grady. Grady skimmed the page for more. *Marriage is the only answer but I will never be able to love that troll.* Grady slammed the book shut.

"Gotta go to town," Grady called as he walked out the door. He harnessed Sam's team and drove them as hard as they could go over rough cow paths.

On the outskirts of town, huge signs read *Spit Spreads Death* and *Obey the Laws and Wear the Gauze.* The streets were empty and as he drove by the school and the businesses, he saw that the windows and doors were boarded up. The Canvas River Hotel was one of the few buildings that still looked inhabited. Grady spotted the doctor's buggy outside and tied Sam's team next to it. Despite the notice declaring the hotel closed, the door opened when Grady pushed. There were several men seated in the dark, not working men from the lumber mill but the brandy-drinking, cigar-smokers who managed it. They weren't likely to be anyone that Grady knew. The erection of the largest lumber mill in the British Empire had resulted in a mass migration to Canvas River. Men from all over were coming and going but Grady's early morning milk deliveries through the bush had rarely forced him to mix with any of them.

Grady scanned the room and found the doctor sitting at the bar. The doctor had aged too. He was wearing spectacles now and he looked lost in a suit that was a bit too big. Maybe he had been ill. Sick or not, Ada needed to be cared for. Yanking the journal from his coat pocket, Grady squared his shoulders for combat. He waved the book in front of Dr. McLean's face.

"What can I help you with, soldier?" The doctor stroked his pointed beard with one hand while holding a drink in the other. Grady tossed the book onto the bar and jabbed it with his finger.

"I've just finished reading my dead wife's diary. It seems you two knew each other really well." The doctor got to his feet and tried to set a placating hand upon Grady's shoulder but Grady shoved it away. "What kind of treatment is this? Is this what women are paying you for? It seems to me that you should be paying them!" Spittle flew through the air as Grady yelled.

The doctor jumped back. "You should go home."

"The rest of Canvas River might be interested in reading all you've been up to." Grady grabbed the collar of the doctor's slack suit to whisper into McLean's ear. "I'll keep quiet if you take care of the girl."

"Why would you want to bring trouble into the community? Aren't we living in enough chaos?" The doctor strained away, clutching his medical bag to his side. "You are the only father that girl knows. I can't take her home with me."

"Then send her somewhere and give her the education you owe her." Grady's nostrils flared as he pulled tighter on the collar.

Suddenly the hotel manager approached the two men. "Excuse me, Dr. McLean, is there a problem?"

"I was just telling the good soldier that he needs to go home. Spanish Flu is rampant in Canvas River."

"And I was telling the good doctor that he has a daughter who just lost her mother and grandfather. She needs a parent." Grady yanked down on the doctor's collar before releasing it.

"This soldier's confused and I am done trying to set him straight. I have hardly slept in days. I stopped in here for a drink to try to settle my mind for a bit and now I have to put up with this." Dr. McLean sighed as he massaged his temples with his fingertips.

"We are not open to the public." The manager's voice shifted to a low growl as he stepped forward towering over Grady. "I'm going to have to ask you to leave."

Metal chair legs scraped across the floor as several patrons rose to their feet. Grady remembered how quickly the men of Canvas River could form a mob, especially when they had been drinking. When he heard someone mutter, "Fucking soldiers brought back the Flu," Grady stuffed the journal back into his pocket before holding his hands up in mock surrender.

"Don't worry. It's simply a case of the good doctor's plague," Grady called, flashing a cold smile. "Half the town's probably been affected." He shoved through the door and backed onto the street.

"I think you've been havin' some troubles." An old man with a big red nose and tiny veins spidering their way over his ruddy cheeks was leaning against the hotel. "I've just the thing for men whose troubles are bigger than they are." A bottle of moonshine dangled at the man's side. Grady accelerated his stride as he crossed the road. He didn't need any more trouble today. He thought he remembered Sam mentioning two sisters who lived in Manitoba. He would have to try to find addresses and write. It would be just his luck that the Flu had carried them off by now too. He was always the one trying to do the right thing but nothing ever turned out the way it was supposed to. He had married a woman who was pregnant with another man's child. He stayed with her even though she refused to be a wife to him. Now he was stuck trying to find a home for her girl. If this is what he got for doing what was right, why should he hold himself back from committing a little wrong? Grady's heels scraped against the gravel as his feet turned back for the bottle.

"Hey, aren't you the milkman? The one whose store burnt?"

"I was," Grady said handing over his money.

*

Grady unhitched and watered the team back at Sam's in the tarnished light of the setting sun. While the horses guzzled, Grady joined them tipping back the moonshine. His throat was numbed to the burn he had felt when he had taken his first swigs while driving home. As he led the team to the barn, he noticed a strange rut trailing across the ground. His eyes followed it, finding Ada hauling Sam's body, her arms under his as she staggered backward. Grady secured the horses and ran out after her. Ada's chest heaved with exertion. Tears strayed down her cheeks tugging dust and dirt with them.

"He's too heavy," Grady said, reaching out to take the body.

"Let me do it," she grunted. "He's my only family".

"You can't just drag him across the yard. It's disrespectful."

"He knew I would have to do it. He already dug the hole and built his coffin. It's in the shed. Mine's in there too. We weren't sure who was going to die from it first," Ada cried, strain cracking her voice.

Grady stumbled to the shed and then stiffened, his muscles forcing his small frame to attention. Of all the shocking things Grady had seen during the war – the monstrous trench rats, school boys carrying grenades in their pockets, comrades blown apart – the sight of the homemade caskets upset him more. Grady shuddered as he imagined Sam measuring himself and Ada for the boxes, lying inside to ensure they fit. The smell of pine bit his nose as he heaved the larger box over his shoulder and carried it to the grave. As soon as Grady positioned Sam inside, Ada pulled a hammer from her apron and began nailing the lid shut. Grady wondered if this self-sufficient child wasn't really a wise old woman disguised as a girl as she pounded her way around the lid in a race with the dissolving sun. In the muddied light, the girl looked so much like her mother – the same surprising ember strands among what at first seemed to be mousy brown hair, the sprinkle of tiny freckles sown across her nose.

When the lid was secured, Grady bowed his head and crossed his hands in front of him. Ada did the same. Grady meant to say a few words but when he removed his hat, no words would come out. "Sorry, I can't speak to God today," he said. As the two of them filled the hole, the soft scrape of dirt against the metal shovels was the only hymn that was sung.

The burial was complete. Ada disappeared in the dull-grey dusk. Grady stepped back to stretch after his exertions and his hand hit something hard and rough: a simple wooden cross with the name Sophia carved into it. It stood alone, propped up against the wind, mimicking his own aloneness in the world. Grady's throat was suddenly tight and dry. He needed to get that bottle. And that journal. And to get out of his stinking uniform. He wasn't a God-damned soldier anymore. Grady marched to the wagon for the bottle and the journal and then he found kerosene in the shed. He carried it all over to the brush pile in the north-west corner of the yard. He doused the dry branches with fuel and then set a match. PHOOOFF! The fire's breath scorched Grady's face as it barked to life. He was going to say goodbye to Sophia, to Sam, to the war, to wanting. He ran to the cabin to get his fiddle. He would serenade the consummation of his former life as his uniform and the journal burned.

His throat scalded with moonshine, he set the bottle down and took the fiddle from her case. His fingers sunk into the small burn marks from cigarettes and traced over the death crack etched in her back from the time she was dropped in a foxhole raid. His rough hand ran over the fiddle's body, her back, her belly, ribs, and shoulders. The wear marks from his jaw and the tiny chips along her worn edges were all part of their story together. Grady tightened the bow, gripped the instrument between his jaw and shoulder, and drew the bow to play her, to make love to her again but the fiddle was dead, her vibrations gone. In his mind, he could hear the melancholy notes of an Irish lament but his fiddle only sounded stuffy. Fiddles that aren't played regularly become stagnate, losing their sound, their heart. This one had gone too long without love. The notes no longer rang out.

"Kindling!" Grady shouted flinging the fiddle onto the fire and the bow in after it. He knew that fire purifies. He let it cauterize the ache. The horsehair blackened and stunk and the strings curled as the fire digested the catgut. The steel E string popped and bounced around after the fire released it from the pressure of being pulled so taut. Flames flickered from the f-holes. Grady held the bottle to his lips again and felt the wanting turn to ash, all that unrequited love burnt up.

Alcohol burns and purifies too. It fills the body with warmth where there was only emptiness. Waiting for Sophia to love him was over. He pulled off his army jacket and fed it to the flames. He tore off his shirt, shedding buttons to the ground and burned that too. Then he tossed in his cap and that wrinkled tie. Grady remembered the Nova Scotia regiment dying on all sides of him as they charged the Pimple at Vimy. He had volunteered to sacrifice himself for a greater good that day before powdering away into dust. He just kept on running and shooting and waiting to die a hero but all he'd managed to do was cause the Germans to waste a few rounds of ammunition. He survived the war, but for what? Please God, don't let it be for a life crammed into a bush shack raising an orphan.

*

Grady's throbbing head woke him. He lay face down in the dirt, the ground festering with the smell of dead leaves defeated by snow mold's rot. He lifted his head to see tiny streams of water struggling for soft places to be welcomed in, the change in season forcing a reordering, a renewal. The empty bottle and Sophia's journal were sunk in the crust of the last remnants of snow and the smoldering brush pile was reduced to charred bones. He shivered now that the blaze that had kept him warm died out. Ada knelt between the graves, dropping handfuls of dirt from one hand to the other, over and over. Grady pushed himself up and staggered to her.

"Who is my father?" she asked not turning to look at him.

"I guess I am." Grady's palm scrubbed over his face. "I guess I'll have to be."

BAD MEDICINE

Louise Bernice Halfe

2020, a dangerous time
as we greet one another
with mask-covered mouths.
I think of residential school
muted voices speaking
through the imaginary duct tape.
This time
eyes crinkle, frowns
are more readable,
we muffle greetings
or lift our hands to hold back
those who are still
barefaced.

Unmasked
with the lurking Covid
just a breath away
waits to invade their lungs.
I wonder what they will do
as they attempt
to receive the blessed wind
guiding down their strangled
passages. I wonder what they
will think as the sun sets
for the last time
into their clouded eyes,

for those who want to walk
into another day
to bundle their grandchildren
into arms that have waited
months for this reunion
we cover our faces,
keep death at bay
for another day.

ODE TO PENELOPE

Maureen Ulrich

You lurk behind the leftovers
in the back of my fridge. Bide your time.

Tuesday night, I place you
on the counter to warm.
You perk and pulse. Expand.
Look at me. I'm ready.

On Wednesday,
you lure me from bed.
I portion your elastic flesh for our next
assignation. Cajole the rest
with flour and water that clings to the crevices
between my fingers.

By mid-afternoon, you overflow
the bowl's rim. I wrestle you into a boule.
Score you with a blade. Thrust you in a hot oven
where your skin browns. Blisters. Breaks.
You emerge triumphant. Fragrant.

Share me with a friend,
you whisper.
I leave your progeny on doorsteps.
Sourdough spreading in mason jars.

BIRDS, SILENCE, WINTER: NOTES

Lorri Neilsen Glenn

It snowed all night. I inhale cool air from the cracked window and listen. So far, no sounds of shoveling.

The sun cuts through the curtains like a promise, and except for the occasional car, the only sounds I hear are soft mumbles and coos of the pigeons and grackles on the roof, the cascading flutters as they drop to the feeder. Chickadees, Canada Jays, sparrows and more—they all seem ravenous this year.

There is no silence like the silence after a snowfall. This year, especially.

*

When I arrived at the Indian grocery store yesterday, the snow was fat, wet and so heavy I could barely see the windows of the pizzeria and the kebab restaurant across the way. I waved at the masked clerk behind the plastic barrier, thinking the new shield must protect him not only from infection but from the blasts of cold air when the door opens. I found the gram flour, finally, after poring over the labels on several varieties: garbanzo, chickpea, gram, besan, chana—which is which? Since we moved to a new neighbourhood, we can walk to shop for groceries. Isolation has given us time to cook foods we have rarely cooked. By the time I left the store, the snow was ankle deep and flakes swirled in the wind like thousands of tiny white wings. Or a cloud of viruses.

I blocked the thought.

*

Studies show birds are vital to our well-being. When we moved, we culled decades of belongings—perhaps *albatrosses* is the better word—and settled in a house half the size of the one we left. We could easily see out the front and back windows and the lockdown gave us the time to watch the world outside. My husband bought bird feeders and dug through stacks of boxes to find a book about Nova Scotia birds. As he watched several species begin to visit our yard, he was soon absorbed: surely this one is a chickadee, but its tail is shorter, is it a nuthatch? Raised on the prairies, we could identify several common birds, but now began to look for nuances we hadn't noticed before. As a photographer who captures the telling detail, he turned his eye to the colours of feathers, the length of a bill. For Christmas of 2020 he asked for a dispenser for seed to more easily refill the feeders and when he opened his birthday gift the following February, he laughed when he pulled away the tissue to find suet cakes. When I found them in the hardware store the week before, I realized two things at once: we could make our own suet cakes—people have for decades, after all—and, like millions of others in the world, we are beginning to focus on, even revel in, the small. A window is a small frame in which to capture a piece of the world; a mind in a pandemic can narrow its focus—at least mine has. Blake's "world in a grain of sand" has become an invocation.

But am I learning to pay better attention? What am I not seeing?

*

In March of 2020, a friend commented on the absence of contrails over her seaside home.

In the city, I heard no planes overhead and at night I saw stars, no blinking lights crossing the sky. Heavy traffic disappeared, leaving the streets open to the sweep of fresh sea air. Ambulance sirens, however, cried in the distance as often as before, especially at night.

*

After the snow stopped, we took the dog over to the Motherhouse grounds. The area was first settled in the late 1800s by the Sisters of Charity and when their numbers dwindled, the Sisters kept their residence but sold the grounds of their 70-plus acre property. Two years ago, the developer razed the grounds, hauled away logs from 200-year-old trees, destroyed cairns and statues, then left the fields to languish. The devastation felt like murder. The area had been an idyllic place to walk through groves of trees, around a small pond, shaded in summer and sheltered in winter.

For decades, crows have flown from all directions across the Bedford Basin to roost at sunset on these lands. Often, up to 9,000 of them gathered, shrouding the trees in stippled black veils. The Sisters of Charity, along with students and instructors at the nearby university, learned to expect the cacophony. When I taught 4:30 p.m. classes, the students and I couldn't hear each other from two metres away.

After the deforestation, the crows seemed to disappear.

But I was wrong. "Crows find a way," said a local academic who had studied the Bedford Basin crows for years. Their sunset gathering was their cocktail hour; they'd gather on the Motherhouse grounds late afternoons but move to neighbourhood trees farther away for the night. Yet I hadn't heard them.

Within a year, green had begun to return in the fields. In summer, insistent saplings were the height of a human and wildflowers and long grasses grew up through the wood chips and rubble. This afternoon, as the sun began to set and we watched the dog roll with delight in the fresh snow, I could hear a few crows call from a small grove of trees at the end of the field. The branches were knuckled with them.

Crow time, I whispered. I've missed you.

*

In 2007, Nova Scotia wildlife experts began to report cases of avian trichomonosis in songbirds, hawks, pigeons and fowl. A parasite that causes death, it is transmitted primarily by bird feeders. The Birds Canada organization recommends we put away our bird feeders during the summer when the disease can spread rapidly. In winter, the parasite lies dormant and birds are less likely to be infected. I wonder how far the parasite has travelled across Canada. The global bird population is already in perilous decline: a news report estimates the planet has lost three billion birds in the last fifty years.

*

During the first few months, I turned to podcasts and YouTube interviews with poets and other writers, voices lulling me to sleep. I was hungry for ideas to push me beyond the here and now, and paradoxically, to force me to be more present. There is a certain relief in contemplating these ideas – they cut through the noise about viruses and variants, a dying planet, political corrosiveness, and more.

A philosopher wonders if we can still talk of beauty and truth in cynical times. A black activist discusses how we can support people of colour in ways that decenter the given. A botanist: what do the lives of trees teach us?

Yet I've spent time, too, searching for answers to random questions, as though any kind of knowledge could crack-fill my crumbling sense of control. How cold is too cold for horses? What's an acceptable level of radon in a house? In the 1950s I'd sucked a sugar cube soaked in the poliomyelitis vaccine, so how does this new RNA vaccine work? What are the best Italian swear words?

And how do birds survive in winter?

I never saw a wild thing sorry for itself – D. H. Lawrence
*

The *rete mirabile*—Latin, for "wonderful net" is a tight network of veins and arteries found in some warm-blooded vertebrates. In winter, birds' *rete mirabile* is tucked into the core of their bodies, creating a counter-current exchange system: blood from their hearts warms the incoming cold blood from the veins. A memory flickers: northern Alberta; oil tank; sub-zero temperatures; my childhood friend, his dare. But birds' feet are tendons and bone; frigid metal doesn't rip their flesh.

*

God sees the little sparrow fall, it meets his tender view—Civilla Martin
*

Later, a vicious storm hit our area, a Maritime special, a combination of heavy snow, ice pellets, freezing rain, high winds and roller coaster temperatures. The night the storm arrived the house shook, the dog stared wide-eyed and then hid. The power flickered, and my sleep was fitful. The curtains were ghosts ballooning by the crack in the window, and ice click-clicked and ticked on the glass and the roof.

*

One evening, after my husband and I watched *Penguin Bloom*, a movie about a partially paralyzed woman who forms a healing relationship with a magpie, I combed internet tunnels to learn several magpies had been trained for the role. These birds are intelligent, can use tools, mourn their dead and mate for life. They can also recognize themselves in the mirror.

Magpies steal food from other creatures and can be bullies. Farmers complain flocks of magpies overtake their yard. CD covers or other reflective objects on a tree or a clothesline can scare them away. Some people plant marigolds to repel them. Some use a squirt gun. In Cree the magpie—*apistikakakes*—is considered an agent of change.

Along with other members of *corvidae*, magpies are trickster figures, messengers of both good and bad fortune.

We have crows in abundance in Nova Scotia, but the last time I saw a magpie was at a retreat in Saskatchewan. *One for sorrow, two for joy.* I'd walk the tree-lined lane to glimpse their bright tails. A local priest walked the lane with a shotgun in his hand, tallying the results of his kills.

(I can hear pushback from frustrated landowners: *you kill mice, don't you?*

Don't be naïve. Someone has to cull these pests.)

Are some pests more deserving of life than others? It's not as though a magpie is food, like a rabbit or a deer. Any hunter I have known respects the kill, some offer gratitude for it, others have ceremony.

*

A recent analysis of over five-hundred research studies found the noise of human activity has affected the population of sea creatures in life-altering ways.

From ships to oil drills to seismic blasts, our noise affects sea animals' feeding and mating, ability to avoid predators, and throws off communication between creatures that rely on sonar.

The pandemic, however, has affected ocean noise. In the waters of Glacier Bay, Alaska, the U.S. National Park Service used a hydrophone to compare ocean noise in 2020 to that of 2018. Using the fourth Friday in May as a marker to compare, they found decibel levels in 2018 had dropped by almost half in 2020.

As I listened to the birds squawking at the feeders this morning, I realized how much they teach me about silence. Their calls are starker now, more present than in the Before Times. What messages do we miss, what voices are muted, when we surround ourselves with noise? Even now, as I chatter about this phenomenon, I am reminded of the poet Wisława Szymborska's words: *When I pronounce the word 'silence,' I destroy it.*

*

A friend who is a single mother and a schoolteacher both homeschools her daughter and teaches online classes and has lived on a precarious income since March of 2020. Our son works at the local food bank and says the demand for food increases weekly. Countless elderly people, without sharing a hand "touch" through a windowpane or hearing a voice over the phone, have been dying alone. Millions across the world live in cramped complexes with their children, exposed to the virus, without technology to access information or schooling. In Canada, remote communities without clean water are at further risk of disease during a pandemic. My aunt in Winnipeg, now 105 years old, is alone all day and can't hear the phone. My cousin, who visits twice a week, says she is losing interest in her daily crossword puzzles and often doesn't eat. On television, a woman waiting for her shot tells a reporter how deeply she mourns the death of her sister who missed the vaccine rollout by a month.

Three for a funeral. One, two, three, three thousand, three million. Deferred. In 1912, the sociologist Émile Durkheim coined the phrase "collective effervescence" to refer to the loss of individuality and the feeling of transcendence that unites people in a ritual, especially in a religious ritual. We all need a way to mark our grief, to gather in an atmosphere teeming with memories of a loved one.

*

Meanwhile, I have been able to indulge in ideas, long walks and the luxury of trying new foods. My husband, son and our dog are my companions. I have shelter, clean water, books and a sea of cyber-faces in small squares whom I connect with, neighbours to call out to as we shovel snow from our steps. I am in a high-risk category, but I have the luxury of hope. At whose expense, though? These times render social and financial disparities in stark black and white, sharp as a magpie's tail. The silence underneath these long months spells trouble.

Spring in the light this week. A flock of starlings has landed in the back yard today and moves its way around the house. I read an article claiming Shakespeare is indirectly responsible for the starling becoming one of North America's worst pests. The bard's praise of the bird may have prompted an amateur ornithologist to import sixty starlings from England in 1890 and release them in New York's Central Park. The current North American population of starlings is over 200 million. I note there is a poem by Robert Hayden called, "A Plague of Starlings," which I intend to track down.

*

Four for a birth. Learning how to live together fairly and compassionately on this planet would be the kind of birth to celebrate in these times. Can we develop, like the *rete mirabile* in the core of a bird's body, 'wonderful nets' in our communities to maintain equilibrium?

Ambulances still howl late at night. I drive by a woman struggling in the snow to board the bus with a toddler, a baby in a stroller and groceries. In the special needs program our son attends, a recent scare required everyone to be tested. When the results came in, our son's face became ashen. He struggled to breathe until he saw the word 'negative.' I understood only then how pierced with terror he has been for a year. *What wasn't I noticing, even close to home? Have I learned anything at all?*

Simone Weil said attention is the highest form of love. A Hebrew saying expresses the hope: "Let there be such oneness between us that when one cries, the other tastes salt."

At this writing, millions hope for a vaccine. Hope. I boil the water for tea and return to the window to wait for birds to perch by the feeder.

I've heard it in the chillest land
and on the strangest sea.

Quotes from Emily Dickinson's "'Hope' is the thing with feathers," Civilla Martin's hymn, "His Eye is on the Sparrow" and the 1780 version of the nursery rhyme about magpies, "One for Sorrow."

FOR IT IS NOT THE SAME RIVER AND WE ARE NOT THE SAME

Medrie Purdham

The year I promised you no two baths alike,
we nightly invented new terms for day's dissolution.

Ice cube toy bath: captive figures melting
out of the ice cubes and into the flows.

Jellyfish bath: the plastic pudding cups
we kept for paint pots inching towards you

on capillary waves as you tittered, their
imaginary sting a vivid prospect. Bath-

in-the-dark, in the thickening dark, just that.
Ceiling-abseiling papery butterflies

utterly falling for you: butterfly bath.
Targets I tagged on a shower curtain,

splat of your water-balloons: lawn-game bath.
I admonished you once for flooding the room,

pressing your foot flat against the faucet,
making a plate-balancer's plate of water.

I'm sorry, you said, but I did love the effect of it.
Your "sorry" was a trill in a glade. I heard "did love"

in the Renaissance way. You cried during umbrella-
in-the-shower bath, its nerve-end tin-roof patter.

Now it's quarantine year, and you turn twelve.
Tall, private, full of headphones. My drive

to show one day's difference from another,
gone. Our knack for making worlds within our walls,

gone. You keep your own hours, up all night.
When morning comes in at the smudged window,

our fingerprints throw light everywhere, wash out
our whole experience. Yet I remember a green bath,

a snowball bath, a starts-with-B bath: alliterative broth
of bowls, bubbles and brachiosauruses,

where a beater chewed the water
as though it were addressing itself

to the most anemic egg. And ebullient you,
whipping up whirlpools, both riddle and force.

KEEPING HIM SAFE

Robert Currie

She wonders what to tell her son.
In grade one, he knows about washing hands
and wearing masks, but physical distancing
makes no sense to him. He loves to wrestle,
loves a good hug, doesn't like her saying
he should only hug his parents.

Keep it simple, she thinks. There's no need
for him to hear about the dangers
facing Grandpa in the care home,
certainly not about people dying there.
Tell him what he needs to keep him safe,
but let him stay just a kid.

A week until Christmas
and they haven't even got the tree up.
The days so short and so much to do.
Right now get him off to school.
Pray there's no Covid there.

She helps him into snow pants
and parka, tugs his winter boots on,
wraps a scarf around his neck, warns him,
"Wear your mask in school,"

and notes his grin. "You hear me, son!"
but he's laughing now. "Sure, Mom.
This is great. Going to school and it's
still dark out. It's like a magic night."

ITSY BETSY SPIDER

Tanisha Khan

Seven months into lockdown, I knew the spider resting on the dining hutch wanted something from me. She was three feet of green and blue carapace that bulged into a silver egg sac. Sometimes she descended and hung impossibly from a solitary thread. Her obsidian legs didn't weave, but they scraped the floorboards when she scuttled across to eat the pickles I left far out of her reach. I was too nervous to get close, though I didn't think she would harm me—she seemed chill. Her eyes watched me, meditative, considering as if I were some funny TV show.

Months back, when she was fuzzy and the size of my pinky nail, I'd thought of killing her many times—considered picking up a shoe and watching her body splat and ooze the way many others had before.

My dad warned killing spiders brought storms, but the prairies so often felt like dry wheat and canola seas; this never seemed a bad thing. So, on those hot summers with each skittering find in the basement, I let waves rush from the sky.

Now, my dad wasn't here to say anything—neither of my parents was. They were too afraid to fly, too frightened to come back home from Chittagong and leave my sick nannu, whose limbs had withered to twigs. On FaceTime, her skin glistened with sweat and fever, like tree bark amid a monsoon, and I found myself whispering prayers I thought I'd forgotten.

But even without my dad, in the early days, when the spider glanced my way, I stayed my hand, let the shoe drop. We were the only two living beings in my parents' house, and since the calls from the few friends I had dwindled to none, and since I could no longer pretend at having friends by going to cafés, attending graduate lectures, or sitting in crowded parks, to outrun my loneliness, the spider—Betsy, I'd decided to call her—became my only company.

Her body shifted with discomfort when I cried, and she drummed her legs on top of the hutch when I stared too long out the window. It was easier for her, I think, since she hadn't known the outside world before we shut ourselves away. I thought about trips to the grocery store but then made my way through the stash of pickled and canned vegetables in the basement instead.

My body thinned. My pajamas hung from my shoulders, billowed about me when I opened the window to let in the wintry air, but I couldn't bring myself to care.

It was on one of these days when I felt exhausted from doing nothing that Betsy spoke.

"Oh, seriously. Just stop your moping and dramatics," she said. "You're such a sad little fly," she snickered.

Too far gone in my loneliness at this point, her voice didn't surprise me. I was affronted; I scowled instead.

"Oh, no, no. Don't make that face. You don't have it so bad. You're alive, aren't you? Safe?"

"Who gave you permission to decide when I can wallow?" I asked.

"Myself, of course. Do you see anyone else here?" Betsy replied. I harrumphed, stuck up my nose, started to walk away. "Yes, that's better," she called after me. "Look alive! Attitttuuudde."

Usually, I lay sprawled across the cold tiles in the kitchen, watching YouTube videos and eating peanut butter out of the jar, wishing someone would phone me or pick up my calls. But after the exchange with Betsy, this felt indulgent.

"Everyone else probably feels similarly, little fly," she said. "It's the winter sads—give them some time, but don't be lazy and gourd-like about it."

I thought then that Betsy was right, that despite never having met the outside world, she was probably the wisest spider I'd met. Winter sads, pandemic sads—wasn't it all similar? I did most likely resemble a squash, sad and lazy in its patch.

"Yeah, yeah, okay," I said. "You're right."

So I turned on a ghost murder mystery podcast for us. Somehow, others' lives, surreal and fucked over as they were, made mine feel less bad, which in turn made me feel a little bad, humbled and guilty even. But then, I thought, wasn't this what it meant to be human? I asked Betsy what she thought.

"All you flies are the same," she told me, and I shrugged. I guess to her, I was an insect too.

I flicked a spoonful of peanut butter onto the wall for her, and she scraped it off, leaving delicate gouges in the beige paint. We hung out this way until I went to bed downstairs and then woke up to follow the same routine.

*

On the ninth month of lockdown, Betsy, who had grown, but hadn't woven at all since I first discovered her, started weaving. I woke up one morning to find her lengthened legs placing the finishing touches on a hexagonal web, iridescent and spanning the entire wall beside the dining hutch. The strands shone, dripping with a liquid that marbled into pearls.

She beckoned with one of her front legs and pointed at the web, a thing that was bigger than even me.

"You want me to touch it?" I asked from afar.

"Yes, little fly," she said and tapped her leg twice in affirmation, the way she used to before she spoke.

"I don't know," I said, "not sure I want to, you know—not that I don't trust you exactly. It's just, well, why should I?"

"Well, little fly, I'm sort of sick of seeing you mope, and since you were wise enough not to kill me, I'm giving you this gift."

"You're gonna eat me?" I asked. And I thought about this, the fact that she hadn't yet, so far. Somehow, even as I said it, it felt untrue.

"No, you aren't the kind of fly that I would find tasty," she said. "I can tell. So, no worries on that account. As I said, this is a gift. Touch it, and you'll leave this place, find the answers to the loneliness you feel."

I considered her offer, the unchanged quality of my days. Though I was starting to feel better about being shut in, there was something burrowed deep in me that gnawed at my happiness—it went further, it seemed, than the missing friends. Really, I thought, life was so screwed up as it was; what harm was there in this? So, I walked to the web. As if to make her intentions clear, Betsy backed away from it and moved further on top of the hutch. I watched as my hand took on a luster similar to the web; this transformation then started to travel up my body, making it disappear. Sounds so constant I'd forgotten them—like the ticking clocks, creaking boards, and humming radiators—slipped away into silence, and just as my vision started to go, and my heartbeat raced, I heard Betsy's voice again.

"Oh, I should mention, you're going to need to think and work to get out of this. Otherwise, you don't really deserve to."

"Wait, what do you mean?" I asked in a panic. I couldn't see her anymore, couldn't move my body.

"It'll help you see your problems truly for what they are," she said. "Kisses! You're Welcome!" And that was the last I heard of Betsy for a while.

*

I was in a space that was full of grays and shadows, with no windows or doors to be seen. In the middle were a bunch of women, perched on stools, in a circle.

"Ah, look, another one of us, come to join! The last one, I think," said one woman.

There seemed to be only one empty stool. I started toward the circle and stopped right before taking a seat, rooted to the spot. That's when I realized all the women were me. That is, they all looked like me, though they were dressed differently, some in styles and fashions I would never consider.

"Yeah, you're probably thinking what we were: Oh, how is this possible?" one of them said. "That's old news, though; don't start."

"Be nice," said another. This version of me wore a long garnet dress as though she were ready for an evening gala. I looked down at my pajamas. "It's all very shocking at first. Can you move again yet?" I walked over to the stool.

"Freakin' awesome," said another me in a leather jacket and biker shorts. "Let's get those deets—was it a spider for you too?"

This time, I found my voice. "Yeah, it was," I said. "So like...what is this?"

"Not too sure, mate. Seems like we're just at her mercy. Got to sit here 'til she lets us out, I guess, the she-devil."

British me sounded sort of cool. But, somehow, even though I felt shaky, it seemed untrue that Betsy really was malicious. Tricksy maybe, but not awful like some devil. At least it hadn't seemed that way in all the months we'd hung out. Besides, Betsy seemed far too elegant and refined for pure malevolence.

"So, come on now, get it all out. Tell us your woes," leather jacket said. She did a dramatic sigh. "What's been keeping you up through your pandemic?" She waggled her fingers and leaned forwards. The others, too, leaned forward, waiting on what I had to say.

All of it had the feel of an AA meeting or what I imagined a support group might feel like.

"Wait," I said, "so you're all me—or we're all each other—but from different lives? Worlds?" They nodded with great patience, as if having already been in my spot earlier by minutes, hours, maybe even days, they'd been afforded some great wisdom. "Right. Okay," I said. "And in every single world, there's been a pandemic?" My voice rose a little at the last word, incredulous over the fact that all versions of my world could be in such a miserable state.

"Yeah, man. It was an inevitability, really. Humans have always been fucked, I think, but they've just fucked themselves over more by not listening to rules, ya know? All it took was some movement across borders, a few masks let loose, and pretty soon, entire countries and states were dying. At least in my world." It was the girl dressed in attire that looked biker chic. Her nonchalance was disturbing.

"So, in this rotten pandemic," said a woman wearing a headband, "what ails you?"

"Well, do any of you feel like you've lost friends or that you no longer have any?" The response I got was a cacophony of angry retorts, shouts, and sad sighs. "Yeah, okay, so I'll take that as a yes. Basically, people forgot I exist."

"Well, we're all here together now, so we can all be frien—" started the girl in the dress, but she was cut off.

"Oh, the drama!" said one of the girls. "That's not even so bad! Try having a pandemic come about and being friendless because your best friend made an even better friend than you."

"Yeah? What about me? My boyfriend left me for someone else in all of this, and now I don't have anyone left because all his friends were my friends. Now, those friendships are too awkward to keep. It's humiliating."

I sighed. "That blows," I said, "but at least it was something as awkward as a breakup that stopped your friendships. I don't think I was in any of my friends' inner circles to begin with."

"No, that really isn't as bad," she responded, and I was taken aback.

The women kept arguing, kept bickering, and speaking over each other. No one's problems, their hurts, were as bad as the others they told one another, and on and on it went. I couldn't think of why Betsy would have ever wanted me to come here, or why any of their Betsy's would have wanted any of these versions of me here—to what end?

I slumped on my stool and thought maybe I could find a small corner to sleep or figure out how to return to my house. The house had seemed so miserable before, so desperately lonely, and yet, being here amongst so many people after so long—something I had wanted, albeit not exactly in this way—felt too tiring. But something kept me fixed to my stool. These girls weren't just people; they were me in other lives, other miserable lives, it seemed. Were we all just destined to be sad and lonely? I didn't see the point of trying to one-up each other regarding our miseries. This was not the sort of social visit I had hoped to get after months of no human interaction. I couldn't take it, the claustrophobia of it all.

"Shut up," I screamed, and they all did.

"Don't be so r…" started one of the women.

"No, zip," I said. "Do you realize how ridiculous this is? No, don't answer. You do, but you'll probably be too stubborn to admit it because, well, you're all me, or different versions of me, anyway, and I wouldn't." I sighed.

The woman in the long red dress raised her eyebrow at me, and I wondered briefly why I hadn't thought to go through the entire pandemic wearing extravagant evening wear. "I know I was the last one here, but don't you think it's all a little weird that we all ended up in a room full of each other only to go at each other's—our own?—throats about which one of us is lonelier? I mean, come on, that's just so fucking sad." Someone sniffled. "You know, maybe *we're* the problem."

"Excuse me, but I am definitely not the problem. Maybe you are in your sad little life, but I…" said biker chick.

"See, that's just mean. Do you speak to everyone like that? I know you can't be entirely right because you are me, and if all of us being here has proven one thing, it's that we seem to think that we are at the centre of it all. I mean, how fucking narcissistic are we?"

"Oh, because you are so much better." One of me crossed her arms.

"I'm not. I believe all of us are lonely. That maybe we don't have the closest of friends, and that sucks right now. I mean, I spent days on the kitchen floor eating peanut butter."

Some of the girls looked at me with judgment. "Yeah, I don't think I need advice from you," one said.

"I'm just saying that maybe even if we don't have anyone close right now, some of it might be us, and not others." Some of the other girls crossed their arms too. "I mean, it isn't totally our fault. But, well, maybe it is okay to be a little sad over this—maybe that isn't so bad. And maybe when we can, we can make more of an effort to listen. If I'm at all like what you've exhibited, then no wonder no one sticks around long enough. Or maybe, it's even that we need to be confident" – I looked meaningfully at the girl whose friends had left her after a breakup – "to be so sure of ourselves, we can approach them first."

I looked around the room, at all the stools knocked over, the girls standing. None of them said anything, but I felt the truth of what I'd said. Slowly, the girls stopped moving, and their bodies became limned in silver, the shade of Betsy's egg sac. Spiderwebs crisscrossed between the girls, and I stood at the centre, in the web. I extended both hands and touched the web's glittering strands. The room and all my other selves started fading to black.

*

I was in the house again, in front of the dining hutch. Betsy hung in front of me on a single string, poised and knowing.

"Well, little fly, that was much quicker than I thought. Maybe you're much wiser than I thought." Her body shivered in a laugh. "Nothing is interesting enough here to keep me. I'm tired of the peanut butter and pickles, and you aren't all that appetizing."

"Do you have to go?" I asked. I didn't know if I was yet ready to hang around the house alone.

"Yes," she said. "But I think you might check your phone." With that, Betsy crawled up the web. She and those iridescent strands winked out of the house as though they'd never been there.

I went over to the kitchen floor, where I had left my phone. I scrolled through and noticed I had a few missed calls, some from my parents and others from friends I hadn't heard from in months. I pressed the call button and listened to the phone ring. I grabbed the jar of peanut butter and spooned some in my mouth. For old time's sake, I flicked my spoon until some peanut butter landed on the wall, and, slowly, it dripped to the floor in viscous droops.

PARADOX

Paula Jane Remlinger

Today is an occasion: leaving the house.
First time in weeks, climbing out
of a fallout shelter after an apocalypse.
The faintest scent of hope permeates,
enlivens the lizard brain, something
unfamiliar after so much time.

Outing to the city: groceries, mail. Do you
have your mask, hand sanitizer, disinfectant wipes?
A good notion of social distancing, a personal bubble
that screams *stay away?* I have dwelt too long apart.
I am the thing that doesn't belong—a strange
newness, unfolding wings in a caterpillar world.

Everything is different. I navigate the unknown.
Worst of all, it *was* once known. I knew these streets,
neighbours, shops. The familiar cadence of daily life, work—
who knew there was such comfort in routine? I don't recognize
myself: a fragile-winged fluttering, tremulous heart.
There is no living in this world, no escaping from it.

WHAT HAPPENS AFTER YOUR TEST

Shannon McConnell

Go home. Take off shoes, jacket, and mask.
Wash hands. Take temperature.

Not all laboratories report results through this website.

Make dinner. Do dishes. Check Twitter.

Refresh
Not all laboratories report results through this website.

Scroll through Netflix. Watch YouTube. Take temperature.

Refresh
Not all laboratories report results through this website.

Text friend. Check email. Scroll through Instagram.

Refresh
Not all laboratories report results through this website.

Scroll through Facebook. Smell candles. Take temperature.

Refresh
Not all laboratories report results through this website.

Listen to podcast. Check email. Take shower.

Refresh
Not all laboratories report results through this website.

Scroll through TikTok. Take temperature.

Refresh
Not all laboratories report results through this website.

Text friend. Pace around apartment. Stare out window.

Refresh
Not all laboratories report results through this website.

Lie on bed. Stare at ceiling.

Refresh
Negative (Covid-19 RNA test)

LEAVING

Miriam Körner

Summer 2019

At first, he doesn't tell her about the dream. Maybe he doesn't think of it when he wakes up in the morning, shutting off the alarm, making breakfast, refilling the dogs' water pails – there isn't much time between the world of dream and leaving the house for work. His half-finished teacup, cold by the time she sets it into the kitchen sink, a common occurrence.

But the dream returns. Not every day – or at least not that he can remember. On Monday, a new detail is revealed in his dream as if he were watching fog lifting, piecing together a landscape bit by bit.

"In my dream," he says on Saturday, the covers warm from their body heat, "we're leaving. We're going to the cabin. Our boat is cramped with all the stuff we're taking. There isn't much room. The dogs are sitting on top of our gear."

She can picture it easily. The 16-foot boat. Thirteen sled dogs straining on too short chains, rubbery noses taking in the shoreline smells, muddy paw prints on grocery boxes. How many times had they gone to the cabin, dogs and all?

He pulls her closer. There is more to his dream. The picture in her head changes. The dogs are cowering now. Ears laid back. Panting. Amongst grocery boxes, frying pans and flowerpots. Flowerpots?

"Why are we leaving?" she asks, suspicious now.

"I don't know. Something has happened. It isn't safe at home anymore."

"What happened?"

"It is just a dream," he says. A picture emerges in her head. On top of the gear: A rifle. Loaded.

*

Just a dream. He'd said the same thing, the morning Frank died. "I had a dream," he said, his breath stale from a decaying tooth. "I dreamed Frank was laying in the grass between here and the dog yard. And the ravens were picking at him."

"And you didn't go out and look?" she asked, casting the covers aside.

"I did. I went out in the middle of the night. He was sleeping. In his dog house."

A feeling of relief. Short-lived. When she did go out, Frank wasn't in his doghouse. He was laying in the grass. Dead. No ravens.

"I had that dream again. The same one," he says on a Thursday. "About us leaving."

"Did you find out what we were running from?"

"People," he says.

"What people?"

*

The dream attaches itself like algae to the shoreline rock. She begins to make lists. What to bring when it was time. Flowerpots. Yes. And dirt. There isn't much on the rocky island by the cabin.

Photos? Definitely. Memories of trips up north by dog team, by canoe. Caribou. So many pictures of caribou. As if her photos would stop them from slipping away.

Books? One box, maybe. Clothes. Dog food. Sleds, harnesses, paddles, canoe. The tent? Yes. Sleeping bags, too. It wasn't safe at home, he had said. They might not be able to return. Camera, she adds to the list, picturing herself taking photos: The small boat barely afloat. The motor pushing the heavy load. She will have to buy extra jerry cans, she thinks and adds them to the list.

She's practiced in making lists. First, for their forages into the Far North. Two lists: One for food. One for the rest. Then to build a cabin. The first one. Up North. On an island on a small lake, far off the beaten path. Lists of 2x6's and constructions nails, plywood sheets and shingles.

Then, she filled the cabin with lists. The first day of freeze-up, the thickness of ice on January 1, the water temperature in September.

That was before 2015. Before the fires.

After the fire, she made two lists. One for the insurance, one for herself. *Things I wish we hadn't lost.* Over the years, the list has become shorter. In the end there was only one thing on the list. And then that disappeared, too. She made a new list. *What remains.* She didn't get around to adding items to the list. They were too busy building a new cabin. This one closer to town. On an island unburned.

*

"I had that dream again," he says after a few weeks.

"And?" she asks.

"It started out the same. We're going to the new cabin with the dogs in the boat. We're staying a while. I don't know how long. Not long. And then we're leaving again."

We're late, she thinks. We're behind. We haven't even left home. "Where are we leaving to?"

"To the burned cabin," he says. "By canoe. The dogs are running on the shore."

She pictures it. Her in the bow, he in the stern. Dogs running through the bush, coming out to the points, trying to reach the canoe. Like that one fall, before the fire, where they went camping with the dogs. How many dogs did they have then? Sixteen? Seventeen? They slept the night by the fire, blue tarp between two trees. Dogs sneaking up on their sleeping bags, curling up in pairs.

How would they get to the burn by canoe? Cross the big lake, down Nemeiben River, then Five Portages up to the Churchill and back down to the lake where their cabin used to be? Or would they stay on the east side of the Highway? She adds maps to her list.

"What about Pepper?" she asks.

"What about him?"

"Was he there?"

"I don't remember."

Pepper. Fifteen. His feet turned outward from arthritis, still wanting to go when they hook up the team. His howl has become coarse over the years, woeful. And still. Pepper is her favourite, ever since his brother Salty died.

"Is he in the canoe?" she asks.

"I am not sure."

"Which dogs were there?"

He counts: "Earl, Grace, Bianca, Ferdinand, Mercedes, Silu, Lucy…."

"The pups, too?"

He nods.

"What about Piranha, Fuzzy, Snoopy and Happy?" She lists the ones too old to run on shore.

"I don't remember."

"Were they in the canoe? You have to remember."

"It was a dream," he says, perturbed by her urgency.

"What happened after?"

"Nothing. We're just there," he says.

"We're staying in the shed?"

"I think so."

They'd pulled out a tiny shack on sled runners. Fuzzy and Snoopy in wheel – they've always been the strongest. Digging into their harnesses, moving the shack foot by foot across the frozen lake. Happy, slower now, still barking each time they'd stopped. When the snow melted, they'd propped up the runners. Brought a mattress and a wood stove. A place to stay. Temporary only. Until they would rebuild.

But they didn't rebuild. The burn a constant reminder of what once was and won't be again. Not in their lifetime. Instead, they'd built the new cabin, the one closer to town.

"What happened next in your dream?"

"I woke up."

"Why were we going to the burned cabin?"

"I don't know. Something bad happened in the world. They were coming for us."

"Who?"

"I don't know. People."

*

Fall 2019

They load the oldest dogs into the truck. Fuzzy, Snoopy, Piranha. Happy pushes through the gate. Pepper wants to come, too.

They look at each other, considering. Maybe it would be best to take them all. Too much, his eyes say, and he pushes Pepper and Happy back to the other side of the gate, where they will wait – fed by the neighbour – with the younger dogs for their return.

During the boat ride to the burnt cabin, she buries her hand in Fuzzy's fur. He cries out when she touches his spine. At the portage, Piranha trots ahead. Lately, she's been staring at them blankly, forgotten who they were. She remembers the portage, though, trots down the path without looking back.

Snoopy hobbles on three legs. The fourth leg almost doubled in size, the cancer a never closing wound. He runs back and forth, chasing scents. He's happy. They all are.

They spend the night at the shack. The dogs tired after the day's journey. Piranha lays in a hollow, half sunken into the ground. It's the dogs' last night, but they don't know it yet. Tomorrow, they will take them to the place, where so many years ago they had camped together, sleeping under the stars. Fuzzy just a yearling then, Piranha's fur shiny in the evening sun. She's chosen the spot. A ridge between two lakes, like a passageway between water and sky.

She lifts Fuzzy's back legs over a dead tree. They lose the trail in the burn. Piranha sits down. Refuses to get up. They've walked too far. The lake, already in sight, feels miles away. He lifts up the old dog, carries her on his shoulders.

"Why do we have to get there?" he asks. She has no reason. Only a feeling. It has to be there. She's come to terms with it. Leaving them there. It can't be anywhere else. They argue and move on.

On the ridge, she builds a fire. From here, she can see the peninsula where they had camped with the dogs. Snoopy's eyes blue like the summer sky. She looks at him now, eyes dull and grey.

She wipes a tiny drop of blood off Fuzzy's eyebrow. The black flies are biting. Fuzzy looks at her, wags his tail. Winces. Snoopy crawls under a spruce with low hanging branches. Piranha stares, accusingly. Eventually, they settle into sleep.

They've talked about it before. Fuzzy will go first. He's the only one who still hears. He loads the rifle. No, she thinks, no. But she does not speak out loud.

The rifle shot echoes from the nearby hills. Piranha doesn't wake before the second shot. Snoopy scrambles to his legs. Fifteen years of trust broken. The dog knows.

He almost can't do it. But he does. Blood trickles onto caribou moss. They leave with three empty shells.

*

Freeze-up 2019
She is restless. If his dream came true, they couldn't travel. Not now. Already, there is ice along the shore.

The dream returns. It starts the same as the others. They are leaving. Twice. Away from home to the new cabin, the one close to town. They stay until they can't. Then they leave again. They make it to the tiny shack in the burn. Rest. But they can't stay. It isn't safe. So they leave again. A third time. Where to go from here?

*

Winter 2019/2020

Just before Christmas, they make it to the new cabin. By dog team. Pepper and Happy inside the sled. Lucy loose behind the team.

The wind is icy, the stovepipe doesn't draft. Smoke from the stove fills the cabin. She opens doors and windows. Hears Happy cry. Since Piranha has gone, Happy has taken her place. She stares at them blankly, whines like a puppy when tied to a doghouse. She lets Happy loose.

The dog tipples around the cabin, paws crunching on snow, paws on the wooden deck, paws on snow, paws on deck. She doesn't notice when the tippling stops.

It would be two days before they find her. A wild chase through the nearby town. Someone has seen her on the highway, in someone's back yard, with the strays on Morin's Hill, begging for food at Keethanow.

He finds her near the bingo hall. Barely able to stand. He carries her back to the island. Happy won't settle down. She seems on a mission to a place she vaguely remembers. Home.

On New Year's Day they move back home. Happy sleeps in her doghouse all day.

*

Spring 2020

On March 14, she meets her sister-in-law outside the grocery store.

"Don't forget to buy toilet paper," the sister-in-law says with a laugh.

"Toilet paper?" she asks, shaking her head.

In the store, the toilet paper shelves are empty.

They'd just come back from a camping trip with the dogs. The previous night, they had slept on a bed of spruce. Dogs curled up around them, their noses tucked under their tails. In the morning, there were fresh caribou tracks over their old trail. She wanted to stay, but they had to rush back. Author readings in Churchill. She'd have to leave early the next day to catch the train.

While they'd kept the fire going at night, 800 km to the northeast an email was sent. The reading was cancelled. She didn't get the message until she was home.

She leaves the store without toilet paper. They still have six rolls at home. Later, she reads a meme on Facebook. "Is anyone else feeling that life was written by a first grader? First there was a virus, then the world ran out of toilet paper and then it snowed."

She orders heirloom seeds on the internet. Feeds her sourdough starter once a day. He buys a fishnet.

She adds seeds to her list before she realizes her mistake. The second time they are leaving they're going north. Just that. North. There won't be any shelter when they arrive, no place to grow a garden. She adds shotgun shells to the list, underlines the two words.

In the evening, they watch a documentary. David Suzuki shows a test tube full of food. A single bacterial cell lives in the tube. It eats, reproduces, eats again. The cells double every minute. After fifty-nine minutes the test tube is half full. Everything seems fine. One more minute, and the tube will be full with bacterial cells, no food, no room to go. We're at the fifty-ninth minute, David Suzuki says.

Life *is* being written by a first grader, she thinks.

*

Break-Up 2020
When the ground thaws they bury Happy. She didn't live long after they'd moved back from the cabin. They'd placed her in the hole they'd dug the previous fall. Covered her with straw and snow. For years now, they have been digging holes in the fall. For the old ones. Just in case. Each time they bury a dog, a part of them dies.

They cover the grave with dirt – still frosty – and add Happy's name sign to the ones already nailed to the big white spruce. The dead dogs outnumbering the living.

*

Summer 2020
Pepper is sleeping on the deck. Lucy next to him. In the dog yard, the others sleep lazily in the summer heat on the roofs of their houses.

They haven't left. On the deck next to her: Flowerpots. The tomatoes – planted too late – are bearing no fruit.

BEFORE THE SOLSTICE

Judit Katalin Hollos

As the lilac blossom blends into the solemn silence of a care home filled with ghost boat-beds and forgotten memories. As the first quince twigs burst into flowers at the same time as rosettes of fever settle on another patient's cheeks. When the long-awaited calmness of the afternoon hours empties into a locked playground with rusty swings wrapped in red and white tapes as some sterile birthday presents. When being light years away from each other is condensed into galaxies of falling almond petals in my window's globe. The new routine of an unfamiliar spring might bring untested habits, the notes of my bamboo flute song growing beyond the five staff lines still fill the deserted parks, and during my usual evening walks, shadows of budding branches still carve their amazing story arcs into the night asphalt as a response to our live-streamed fates.

Someone with a clumsy schedule that knows no boundaries may take comfort in the irregular, trembling rhythm of those mind-blowing fan dances that I can now practise for my own temporary eternity. There are no teachers or audiences, just the four walls of a cardboard box-room. Someone who never ever seems to get anything right may still fit into the annoyingly high-pitched, borderless display of sounds of a so-far silent gayageum zither exiled in a cobweb-covered corner. Being unselected as some bird species that went extinct millions of years ago may now be described with various shades of musical tones the world has never heard. Dreams of youth – the rugged peaks and valleys of troubled relationships ingrained in our souls. The grey gnarled birches on the hill slope we used to run around as playful thirteen-year-olds. We dreamed as many of these remarkable creatures, twisted into countless intricate shapes, as our wildest imagination could come up with. Some were young maidens running from villains chasing them, others may have been miserable souls desperately uttering their last cry before assuming a wooden form and getting forever trapped inside the heartwood. All this existed of course within the realm of fantasy as the future looked ever so bright and we all thought adulthood had magnificent adventures in store for us. The glow of past summers between branch scars.

It's finally time to fulfill all those life-altering promises, but suddenly there is no place to go to make up for the lost mother-daughter plans. I could at last visit *her* more often, but it's only a screeching doorbell, a stuffed shopping bag and our fingers pattering on the window glass that remains for a distant grandmother and granddaughter.

It's like being locked inside my own mind, in a library of faint, pastel-coloured recollections. What it felt like on an icy trail clinging into *their* arms as a kid. How the June trails we tread crunched under our feet as we were looking for blue milkweed beetles, hiding in the last patches of beech forest. How it felt to finally reach the medieval viewpoint, gazing down into the bright twilight valley. How our repressed giggling mingled with the dull rumble of an oncoming copper tram in the sleepy city at our feet. The small snail fossils imbedded in the limestone of the surrounding cliffs – a whole constellation of empty seashells on the rocky canvas.

For days and weeks, I tend to drift through dreamscapes that feel familiar, even though I have never visited them. Fictitious friends show up, stating we have studied in the same class but I can't seem to remember a single moment from their far-fetched claims. It's like waking up in a remote corner of the earth and for seconds not being able to figure out where I am, like returning to the mirror maze of a sleepy northern town I often used to visit during my youth in the light autumn drizzle. The relentless rattling of a red and white cogwheel railway snailing through its hills slightly reminds me of childhood excursions. Gazing down into a valley dotted with tiny, medieval houses makes me recall fragments of my birthplace.

Seasons come and go, but the song of spring-bearing plovers always arrives delayed for some reason. At some point, just as my journey would come to end, I suddenly realize I should not be away from my loved ones, but at the same time, I instinctively feel there is no point in ever going back to my hometown, even though I don't recognize anyone on the silent streets and scentless parks, filled with distant voices that appear to trickle from the pages of decade-old photo album. My thoughts slowly get ladened with remorse. I have now all the time in that small world that I call home these days, but what if one day I fail to wake up? What if I notice I'm stuck fast in its globe, not being able to return anymore? What happens to those who always come late and miss even the chance of meeting themselves? Frozen in a moment, I suddenly realize I should not be away from my loved ones. It may not make any sense ever going back but I still decide it's worth it to make an attempt.

A SCENE FROM "THE PROMISED LAND"

a play

Dwayne Brenna

The not-too-distant future, during a pandemic. The set is the kitchen of an old farmhouse. It might look like a Depression-era farmhouse except that the ratty furniture is of a newer vintage.

Scene One

Morning. Gordon supports Celeste as they enter. She is grimy even though her clothes are comparatively new and fashionable. Having tripped and fallen in the underbrush, she is limping. Gordon helps her to a chair by the kitchen table.

GORDON

That's it. That's right. You just sit right there.

He draws the blinds on the kitchen window.

Let me get you some cool fresh water.

He goes to the sink and pours water from a pitcher into a chipped coffee cup.

That's cool fresh water there. Right outa the well. Best water in Saskatchewan, my grandfather used to say. Got a little sediment now but still it's good to drink.

He gives her the cup, then sets up his own chair ten feet away from her.

You go right ahead and take a swig. Not too much, too fast. You can choke on water, that's a fact.

She guzzles the water. He takes the cup, goes to the sink and refills it.

There's more where that came from.

He hands her the cup. She drinks more slowly. He sits again.

You take your time. Everything is gonna be alright.

She doesn't speak.

Lucky you found your way to shelter before the sun got too high. These summer days'll burn you to a crisp.

She doesn't speak.

Looks like you skinned up your arm real bad. You'd better wash that off. Or else infection might set in.

He gets a bowl from the cupboard and fills it with water. He sets the bowl and a dishcloth on the table in front of her. She begins cleaning her wounds.

That's a nasty cut right there. You musta been scrambling through some kind of underbrush to get a cut like that. What were you running from, I wonder?

She doesn't respond.

No need to talk about it now. I'm sure it musta been bad. I'm sure you wouldn't be here if it wasn't something bad.

He inspects her arm.

I'll get you some iodine.

He goes into the bathroom and comes out, moments later, with a small bottle. He slides it over to her. She winces as she applies the iodine.

Stings a bit, don't it?

                    CELESTE

Lost.

                    GORDON

I know.

                    CELESTE

Out there.

                    GORDON

You're safe now.

                    CELESTE

I was lost out there. In the trees.

                    GORDON

There ain't too many trees out there.

                    CELESTE

Picking berries.

                    GORDON

By yourself?

                    CELESTE

Yeah.

                    GORDON

Where?

                    CELESTE

The river.

                    GORDON

No woman should be out there alone. Not in these times.

                              CELESTE
I know.

                              GORDON
You're not sick, are you?

        *Celeste takes a passport from her coat pocket. She slides it across the table
        to Gordon.*

What's this?

                              CELESTE
Passport.

                              GORDON
Hmm. And you carry it with you, pickin berries.

                              CELESTE
The soldiers.

                              GORDON
What's your name?

                              CELESTE
Celeste.

                              GORDON
Celeste. That's a pretty name. Celeste who?

                              CELESTE
Burton.

                              GORDON
Burton? Celeste Burton? Ain't nobody named Burton living near
to here.

CELESTE

No.

GORDON (*handing her the passport*)

Where do you come from?

CELESTE

West of the river.

GORDON

What do you do for a living, west of the dried-up river?

CELESTE

Farm.

GORDON

Is that right?

CELESTE

Yes.

GORDON

How'd you get yourself lost? That river used to run pretty much north and south.

CELESTE

I couldn't find any berries.

GORDON

That ain't surprising.

CELESTE

I walked.

GORDON

Where'd you walk?

CELESTE

I saw some bushes.

GORDON

And you got lost.

CELESTE

I walked all night.

GORDON

You were out all night?

CELESTE

The sun came up. I saw your house.

GORDON

Good thing too. Army's out there all the time now.

CELESTE

Yes.

GORDON

Folks are tryin' to get out of the city, I guess. Everybody's afraid of the Zed.

CELESTE

What do the soldiers do?

GORDON

Whatta they do?

CELESTE

With the people?

GORDON

You don't wanna know. They can't get close to sick people. That's what they like to tell you anyways. And it's too much trouble to take 'em back to the city.

CELESTE

I see.

GORDON (*getting to his feet*)

Where's my manners? I don't suppose you've eaten anything since yesterday.

CELESTE

I'm fine.

GORDON

Ain't gonna stand by and watch a lady starve to death right here in my own kitchen.

CELESTE

I'm not starving.

GORDON (*going to the cupboard*)

You need a decent meal. That's plain as day.

He finds a knife and takes a loaf of bread from a breadbox on the counter and begins to slice.

CELESTE

Bread?

GORDON

Homemade.

CELESTE

And yeast?

GORDON

I'm a bit of a hoarder. Got yeast til the cows come home. And enough toilet paper to last an army regiment about a year. After that, it's gonna be dry leaves, I'm afraid.

He puts the slice of bread on a plate and gets a pitcher of fresh milk from the fridge. He places them on the table in front of Celeste.

Bon appetit! Oh, and one other thing!

He goes to the cupboard and pulls out a crock of brown sugar.

Demerara sugar! From my own private stash.

She sits, looking at the plate.

I've forgotten the cutlery!

He gets a knife and fork from a drawer, places them on the table in front of her.

CELESTE

Thank you. *(after a moment)* I'm sorry. What do I do with this?

GORDON

You've never eaten bread and milk before? It's delicious. You pour the milk on top of the bread. Then you sprinkle on the brown sugar.

She pours milk over the bread, sprinkles brown sugar on top. Gordon watches expectantly. She picks up the knife and fork and begins to eat.

CELESTE

Mmm.

GORDON

Didn't know nothin' about baking when I first got married. Emily taught me how to bake bread.

CELESTE

Your wife?

GORDON

She was. God rest her soul.

CELESTE

I'm sorry.

GORDON

The Zed, you know.

CELESTE

But you survived.

GORDON

I'm a tough old bird. (*pointing at her plate*) That's Emily's bread recipe right there.

CELESTE

It's good.

GORDON

I used to love it when she baked bread. The whole house smelled like Christmastime.

CELESTE

When did your wife…?

GORDON

It was during that first fall. When the pandemic came. I was riding combine day and night. Such a to-do about everything. I just had to get the harvest done. Out there day and night. Nothin' was more important than that. Didn't even notice that my wife was gettin sick.

CELESTE

So sudden.

GORDON

She said, at suppertime, she had a headache. "Don't worry," she said, "I'll bring you your coffee at midnight." But she didn't come at midnight. She didn't come at all.

CELESTE

I'm sorry.

GORDON

Seems like I did a lot of things wrong back then.

CELESTE

You mustn't think that way.

GORDON

Well. The mind goes where it wants. (*changing the subject*) That bread isn't half-bad, even if I say so myself.

CELESTE (*eating again*)

Didn't think I'd ever taste good bread again.

GORDON

And the milk? That's fresh cow's milk.

CELESTE

It's lovely.

GORDON

Used to have a hundred head of Charolais out there in the pasture. Before the grassland turned to cinders. Now we're down to five cows and a heifer.

CELESTE

We?

GORDON

My son and me.

CELESTE

You have children?

GORDON

Well, they ain't kids no more. There's Rob. That's my son. And I got two daughters. They can't come to visit me now.

CELESTE

Does your son live here?

GORDON

Yeah. He's gonna take over this farm when I'm done.

CELESTE

Where is he now?

GORDON

Out there checkin' his snares.

CELESTE

Snares?

GORDON

He snares rabbits. They taste like chicken if you cook 'em right.

CELESTE

Where does he put his snares?

GORDON

Out there in the thicket. Somehow those rabbits figured out a way to survive. (*He points at her plate.*) Would you like another slice of bread?

CELESTE

You've been so kind already.

GORDON

I'll get you another slice. Ain't everyday you find a girl out wandering through the fields.

He slices the bread at the cupboard and brings a couple of slices to the table on a smaller plate.

Try that on fer size.

CELESTE

Thank you.

She resumes eating. Gordon goes to the window.

GORDON

I'm surprised you didn't see my son out there. He usually sets his snares in the scrubland.

CELESTE

Maybe he was in another part of the pasture.

GORDON

Yeah, maybe. He should be coming home any minute now.

CELESTE

Do you want me to leave?

GORDON

No. But I should tell you a little bit about my son.

CELESTE

It's none of my business.

GORDON

Well, you're gonna meet him. And you should know. Don't get me wrong. He's a good kid. Emily and me, we raised our kids right. Gave 'em a sense of right and wrong. Taught 'em to respect themselves and others. But you can't predict what life is gonna do to people. Even to your own kids.

CELESTE

This pandemic has put everyone on edge.

GORDON

It wasn't the Zed. It was that stupid war.

CELESTE

Your son was in the war?

GORDON

You know how they are when they're young and headstrong. They don't think nothin's gonna hurt them. Figger they're made of steel.

CELESTE (*getting up*)

I should really go.

GORDON

No, no, my dear. You just stay put.

CELESTE

I should really be getting back.

GORDON

That dried up riverbed is a good six miles away. And it's dangerous for a woman to be out there alone.

CELESTE

I'll be all right.

GORDON

That's nonsense. (*He stands in front of the door.*) You just sit right back down. When Rob comes home, he'll escort you at least as far as the river.

CELESTE

I don't want to be any trouble.

GORDON

You can't go out there. Those soldiers shoot first and talk later.

CELESTE

Okay.

She sits down again.

GORDON

And I haven't finished feeding you up yet.

He points at another slice of bread. Celeste forks it on to her plate and eats.

CELESTE

You're very kind.

We hear footsteps at the front door.

GORDON

He's not gonna hurt you or anything. He just behaves a little strange from time to time.

Rob enters, carrying a dead rabbit. He stops inside the door.

ROB *(to Celeste)*

Who the hell are you?

GORDON

Now, Rob....

ROB *(to Gordon)*

You brought her in here?

GORDON

She was outside all night.

ROB

You brought a stranger into this house?

GORDON

She ain't a stranger.

ROB

She ain't a stranger?

                    GORDON
No.

                     ROB
What is she then?

                    GORDON
She's a farmer, just like us.

                     ROB
How do you know that? How do you know, old man?

                    GORDON
She told me so.

                     ROB
And you believe her? She could be telling you anything.

          CELESTE (*getting up again*)
I could just go.

                    GORDON
You can't go out there!

                    CELESTE
If I'm making trouble here.

                    GORDON
You'll get yourself killed.

                     ROB
Let her go.

                    GORDON
It's broad daylight out there now.

ROB

That's her problem.

GORDON

It's everybody's problem!

ROB

She found her way here. She can find her way back.

GORDON

Think about it, son.

ROB

She's got nothin to do with us.

GORDON

She won't survive out there. Think about it.

ROB *(after a pause, to Celeste)*

He's right. It's dangerous out there now.

GORDON

We'll get you out of here in the dark. When it's safe.

Rob finds a chair, turns it backwards, and sits some distance from Celeste, facing her.

ROB

What are you runnin' from?

CELESTE

I'm not running from anything.

GORDON

She comes from the other side of the river.

> ROB (*to Gordon*)

Oh, be quiet! She could be saying anything, and you'd believe her. (*to Celeste*) Are you sick?

> CELESTE

No.

> GORDON

She's not sick. She showed me her passport.

> ROB

Her passport?

> GORDON

Yeah. Ya know, one of them new government issued passports. The ones they give you if you've had the disease and got over it.

> ROB (*to Celeste*)

You've had the Zed?

> CELESTE

Yes.

> ROB (*holding out his hand*)

Let me take a look.

> *Celeste takes a passport from her coat pocket and hands it to Rob. He looks at the passport, then hands it back to her.*

These things are a dime a dozen. There's folks in the city counterfeiting these things all the time.

> CELESTE

It's not counterfeit.

> GORDON

It's not counterfeit, son.

ROB

You don't know that, dad!

GORDON

Now Rob, you gotta trust somebody.

ROB

No, that's just the point. You don't gotta trust nobody. Until they've earned your trust.

CELESTE

If I'm that much trouble, I'll happily go away.

GORDON (*to Celeste*)

You just sit right there. Me and my son'll talk this out. (*to Rob*) She could hardly stand up when she got here. I almost had to carry her into the house.

ROB (*to Celeste*)

You're from the other side of the river?

CELESTE

Yes.

ROB

What are you doin' over here?

CELESTE

I got lost.

GORDON

She got lost, pickin' berries.

ROB

Let me look at your hands.

Celeste holds out her hands.

Palms up.

She turns her hands palms up.

Don't see no berry juice on those hands.

> CELESTE

I couldn't find any berries.

> GORDON

She couldn't find no berries. That's why she came up out of
the riverbed.

> ROB

Can you just shut up and let her answer?

> GORDON

No, I can't shut up. Not in my own house. Not in my own house which I
built with my two hands.

> ROB *(ignoring him)*

That's a pretty fancy coat for a farm wife.

> CELESTE

I bought it in the city. Years ago. Before they locked everything down.

> GORDON

You see? Her story adds up.

> ROB

She's got an answer for everything. That's for sure.

> GORDON

We are good people, son. Righteous people. Now's the time to show
folks who we are.

ROB (*to Celeste*)

How were you planning to get back home? There's army patrols all over the place out there.

GORDON

I told her you'd escort her back as far as the riverbed. When it's safe.

CELESTE

If I can wait here until nightfall and you point me in the right direction, I'll find my way home by myself.

ROB (*considering this*)

I don't like it. You come in here. You could be carrying the Zed, for all we know. (*pointing to his father*) This old man is at risk. He's seventy years old. He's got a heart condition. If he catches this disease, he's a goner.

GORDON

I ain't gonna catch the disease. If I was gonna catch the disease, I would have had it by now.

ROB (*to Gordon*)

You can't be sure, dad. They're sayin' you can catch it more than once.

GORDON

Well, I ain't gonna catch it from her.

ROB (*to Gordon*)

Don't you wanna live no more?

GORDON

I don't wanna live in a world where nobody can be trusted. I don't wanna live in a world where you're afraid to help somebody who needs your help.

ROB (*to Celeste*)

Well, you're here now. Sittin' in this kitchen. There's nothing I can do about that. And I suppose it's not gonna do any more harm to let you stay until nightfall. Once it's dark, I'll walk you back to the river.

CELESTE

You really don't have to. I can make my way alone.

ROB

Well, one way or another, we'll get you out of here. (*He gets up and retrieves the dead rabbit, takes it to the cupboard and finds a knife.*) And another thing: once you're gone and at home safe, we don't ever wanna see you back here. Ever.

He begins to skin the rabbit. Blackout.

SOMETHING FOR YOU AND NOTHING FOR ME

Deidra Suwanee Dees

a little brown boat to go fishing in the sea
to catch   something for you
                and nothing for me,
a white house on a hill, Cadillac with a key
provided   something for you
                and nothing for me,

living our lives in sly hypocrisy
gained   something for you
                and nothing for me,
when I cried out for help in deep despondency
you took   something for you
                and nothing for me,

raping my worth and human dignity
fulfilled something in you
                and nothing in me,
hoping to be loved, waiting endlessly
to reverse   something for you
                and nothing for me,

covering your crimes in silent secrecy
hid   something for you
                and nothing for me,
at last you have died from Covid-19,
now there's   nothing for you
                and something for me

OUT WITH THE LAUNDRY

Elena Bentley

You and her. A kiss. A bra strap
slipped. You and her. Fingers weaved.
An experiment on first base. Fast
forward. Him and her. A wedding.
A baby. *His & Hers* towels. Family
photos on the front porch. Photographer
on the street: Covid-19. Two makes
three. Rewind. You and her. Awkward.
A conversation. No one knows. You
write. Hide secrets inside your poetry.
Even you believe it. You with him.
A wedding. No baby. Stuck at home.
You swipe through her Instagram posts.

Press *like*. The only thing you can like.
Don't leave a comment. Wonder—
will you ever fold *Hers & Hers* towels?

PEDALOGUE FOR A WONKY YEAR

Lloyd Ratzlaff

Wonky: unsteady, shaking, awry, wrong. What to do with such a year?

I write, and I walk, though at seventy-four with an ailing spine and enough non-pandemic issues, there's no further traipsing the riverbank for half a day and coming home more braced to write than before.

I do what I can. No masks required on a pedalogue, no social distancing on trails where flora and fauna do what they've done forever. As in other years, threats and fears of death, my antidotes of reading and writing to get going in the morning (which luckily can also be done in bed when necessary), and the medicine of Ruby and Finnegan, our two West Highland Terriers who can travel to nirvana and back in a minute.

Pedalogues are for noticing and pondering, and the rhythm of the walk often brings on aphorisms like this one from a grandmother I know: "Separate the buckwheat from the bullshit."

January

New year. Some days risen from the dead, others crawling back to the tomb. This morning Sol inhales fog through his nostrils while hoarfrost clings to the trees.

Church sign: "If God had a fridge, your picture would be on it." Another: "Too Cold to Change Sign – Message Inside." In the news a politician says this about arts funding: "We need a certain amount of eyeballs watching."

Bruce Lockerbie: "Art is never satisfied to be an avocation, a resort for dabblers or a refuge for the timid. If it is true that time spent in writing is time lost for earning wages, then it is also true that time spent in writing is time redeemed from its wastedness in mere wage-earning."

Art against bullshit.

February

Inflow, influence, influenza – the words derive from "a belief that epidemics were due to the influence of the stars."

I once worried that others would see me mumbling to myself while out walking and trying to make an art of my inner quarrels. Now they're too busy texting to notice, cross intersections without looking up, or themselves talking into invisible devices. Even in the local bar a guy in a toilet cell unrolls paper while speaking on his cell, *Hey, whatsup, are you comin over or what?*

Zen proverb: "Sin and blessing are all empty. The snake swallows the frog. The toad sucks up the worms. The hawk eats the sparrows. The pheasant eats the snake. The cat catches the rat. The big fish devours the smaller one. And everything is all right. The monk who offended against the commandments does not fall into hell."

The wind can't know how far it will blow, or what it will mark on the way.

March

I take my words for a walk with no money in my pocket, and spy a nickel on the ground. How did I see it among all the waters of spring?

A few more steps and there's a dime.

Finance minister: "The reality is there's substantial global uncertainty right now. We're going to continue to make an active assessment of where we are." Commentator: "There's a downside to the growth forecast." Much human activity cancelled in an epidemic, disclosing its unessentiality.

Once it was said that the human nose provides evidence of the Creator's designing skills, so perfectly shaped to support spectacles. Ruby and Finnegan's noses are designed to snub such human bullshit, bunkum, claptrap, flimflam, hokum, and trumpery.

Heading home, another nickel on the path. I'm twenty cents richer than before. Crossing the schoolyard, also a red pen – into my pocket with the coins, and home to cross out my bad words.

Blackflies one day, butterflies the next.

April

A voice in a dream said: "Either reason takes up the process of observing art and artistry to fathom what is going on there, or the artistic urge takes up reason and tosses it about like a silly plaything."

Epidemic evolves to pandemic, cloven-hoofed Pan ever virile. Isolation, self-protection, maskings and hand-washings – on an individual scale it would be called obsessive or paranoid.

Yesterday the Thunder Beings returned. Today has new crocuses. The sky is a beauty with an ache, shy clouds and tender blues.

I had a good look at the bird whose song never repeats, listened for fifteen minutes with the creature in full view. Long beak, russet crown and back, striped throat and breast, dark patches on wings, doing with its voice what I'll never do with mine. It clung to a willow branch tossing in the breeze, kept singing however the blow. If I name that bird, I'll never see it again.

May

A scientist on the news says we are "stunningly ignorant" of how viruses mutate. James Joyce's old man says, "Ah, there must be terrible queer creatures at the latter end of the world."

On a warm spring afternoon the school buzzer sounds, though playground and parking lot are deserted. Once I heard a teacher summon her students from these swings and monkey bars, "Come on, let's go, it's gym time!" – back to the brick schoolhouse with artificial light and stale air. Now the kids' worlds have shrunk to the size of computer screens.

"Moving forward" – standard escape clause so beloved of politicians, going ahead while back-pedalling, famous Michael Jackson move. A journalist says, "At the end of the day, Washington needs to move forward today."

Bluejay halts my stride and gives me an earful, lifts me from my skull to prove how much bigger the world is than a human head.

June

One day Chuang-tzu and a friend were walking along a riverbank. Chuang-tzu said, "How delightfully the fishes are enjoying themselves in the water!" His friend said, "You are not a fish, how do you know whether or not the fishes are enjoying themselves?" Chuang-tzu said, "You are not me. How do you know that I do not know that the fishes are enjoying themselves?"

The South Saskatchewan flows north, but today's wind drives the whitecaps south, proving that a river can flow two ways at once. A duck takes off, more propeller than wing.

Theodore Roethke: "Art is the means we have of undoing the damage of haste. It's what everything else isn't."

July

Thanks to the beauty who danced beside me until the alarm rang me up. Thanks for her flavour and scent, for the innocence making her lovelier still. For all she offered that I couldn't take, thanks. The thought counted.

Newscaster: "The Maple Leaf plant is completely non-operational and is fully de-contaminating."

I walked a mile in my shoes, and what did the chickadee say? *Deedeedee* (and maybe one *dee* more). If I weren't in the bird's mind it would fly straight through my head.

An ant and a lady-bug nearly collided on the sidewalk, so busy with their business.

August

Salem country church cemetery. Jackrabbit bounds up from behind Uncle Bill's headstone and lopes to the far corner of the churchyard, where the men's toilet once stood in my childhood. I recall an African myth that the hare's lip was split as punishment for saying we shall *not* be renewed like the moon.

Woodrow Woodpecker startles my insides out. A termite under the pine's bark hears a great knocking and doesn't know it's on the verge of becoming a woody. Just so, I expect a knock on the walls of my imagination, to become I don't know what.

How slight the bones of a bird, how full of wind its feathers.

September

I am – therefore I have a right to be. Same for seventy-seven crows in the park also caught in a worldwideweb, but without problems. Cheeky, but no vanity there. Do they live in vain?

Plato's philosopher is "always occupied with the practice of dying." This puzzling self, its cut-to-pieces-ness, living and dying the same gerunding between grumpiness and gratitude. Maybe death is the sincerest form of resting one's case. No race when the wheel stands still. Yet I bump my knuckles even learning to keep a healthy social distance from myself.

Garter snake head-and-tube, long green bean in a bush.

October

Sculptors and carvers leave messes in their workshops, but does anyone care?

Writers suffer the threats of Judgement Day, every idle word accounted for, every adverb, every goddamn preposition, as Truman Capote might have said. Writers are obliged to tell the difference between fiddling around and farting around, even if only to themselves.

Limerick by Lloyd: *Ha haha ha haha haha / ha haha ha haha haha / ha haha haha / ha haha haha / ha haha ha haha ha HA!*

Robin sings and the tailfeathers dip, wings lift when it gives a shit.

November

Is it television networks or evangelists who are more dedicated to bad news?

A chief physician says: "Don't panic, there will be enough vaccine to vaccine everybody who wants." Should I feel secure when a doctor doesn't know a noun from a verb?

Acetaminophen relieves pain and fever. Acetylsalicylic acid relieves Fever and Pain (capitals). Ibuprofen is Pain Reliever/Fever Reliever. So I ask for Fever Reliever, and when I'm in Pain please add Acetaminophen and/or Acetylsalicylic acid.

Or a massive placebo, M-PLAC: *Just one per day may be enough.*

In the egg that hatches, an updraft. In the bird that flies, a stone.

December

Ruby and Finnegan sniff at yellow news in the snow. When it's too cold to walk outside, they chase a ball down the hall and leave a fart behind. We tell them they're good dogs, and they yawn, giving us this day another barrel of laughs and prescribing for me another dose of words.

Then our Tweedledum and Tweedledee agree to have a battle. She shows him who's who, he shows her what's what – a conk on the noddle, a yelp, and back to the game.

New Year's Eve, eldering body another year older and mind hoping to write some words worth reading, even if only in an hour's escape for those to whom Pan hasn't been as gentle. And if pandemonium becomes bedlam, I'll feel blessed to write and read as I can.

Zen prescription for what ails us: Practise for another 3.145926 (or so) years.

A BROKEN BRANCH MORNING

gillian harding-russell

It was a morning with broken branches
gnarled arms across the icy path,
snow drifted in an elaborate conch shell
blocking the southeast corner
of the sidewalk...

The night window I walked up
to, in the rush of dreams
the roar of a train crashing
through blackness on its one-
tracked course having
woken me up to whirling grey,
snow hazing the dark
as the wind lashed and

with this tumultuous scene
held still inside a noisy frame
behind glass in the creaking ship
of the house, my thoughts travelled
back to 4 o'clock the afternoon before –

we had heard the crinkle of plastic bag
over the portable phone as the receiver
was held up to your (listening?) ear,
silence, and then a wispy breath
as we spoke into the empty air
to fill the minutes, hoping the sound,
the rosiness of our voices, a word or two
might sink through the grey densities
of thickening inner weather.

I could picture your old eyes blue
as summer, eyelids delicate as the dead
butterfly wings you find stuck
to the grass, looking out at what was so far
from familiar…life's growing strangeness
growing intolerable, I worried.

Baffled, perhaps, by the one standing
beside the bed, a strange bird
behind a clear visor, not unlike Joan of Arc
in see-through armour while those in white rushed about

the room, but your eyes, the nurse kindly assured us
on speaker-phone, were open – wintry blue, frozen,
in a stop-motion thought, I wondered…but no, she said,
you were so far holding your own.

> An ancient hominid of late middle
> age (old for then) unearthed:
> his skeleton parts gnarled with arthritis,
> spurs in his ears so the archaeologist
> vouched he couldn't probably hear

> but mustn't somebody have loved him
> to keep him alive inside the cave
> away from the wolves, their rising song
> on the shrill-chill edge of a nerve?

And then that broken-branch morning, I knew it
before I learned it later that white morning – you were right now
wandering into the whip of those tangled branches, having heard
the wolves' irresistible lean call…

SOCIAL BUBBLE

Shelley A. Leedahl

If Joey could see himself he'd probably make some joke about how ridiculous he looks, how the respirator's a strange kin to a gas mask. Hang on, no he wouldn't: he can't talk. Or eat. I squeeze the bones of his hand, get no response. Medically-induced coma: he may not even realize I'm here.

I did some research before I went to see him in Vancouver the first time: the endotracheal tube's inserted through his mouth and extends into his windpipe; the nasogastric tube's fed through his nose into his stomach. Jesus. Googling this shit is one thing, standing beside my disappearing boyfriend's bed in a sterile corner of a city hospital while this noisy machine pulses oxygen into him is next level crazy. And holy Auschwitz, he's skeletal. He's as good as dead already.

*

"We're all going to get it anyway," Bren said into the semi-dark of the studio apartment. In the candlelight you couldn't tell that the moss-green scarf reigning in her mountain of dreadlocks was the same hue as her eyes, but I knew it was. "Let's just get it over with, and get on with our lives," she said. "Bring it on, baby."

I've known her since we were eight and in surf school together—girlfriend's always been a daredevil. First to catch a wave at Long Beach, first to have sex (she'd just turned fourteen, and was curious), first to snort coke, first to shack up. Her mom claimed Bren was conceived in a driftwood hut on Chesterman Beach. Claire's an anti-vaxxer and conspiracy theorist. You know what they say about the apple and the tree, eh. Thing is, Bren's so damn charismatic. She doesn't suffer from anxiety or depression, like half the world, and we all count on her to plan the next wild adventure. I call her Sister. And I love her like one.

Bren and Dalen had just started living together, mostly out of economic necessity. There was hardly room for anything more than their futon and a few pillows on the floor. The craft brew pub they worked at shut down last year—Tofino's a tourist town, and it collapsed faster than an old growth forest—and we're all existing in the altered universe that began almost two years ago with a tremor and rumbled across the globe with tsunami force. Half a dozen people I know have built shacks in the deep dark woods with tarps and deadfall, like *that* will save anyone from the virus. A growing number are exiting on their own terms: it keeps the paramedics hopping.

My personal low point—before Joey's infection—was when Covid-19 mutated and started spreading through dogs, then the first cases of dog-to-human transmission were recorded somewhere in the Middle East. It's just so weird not to see tongue-lolling, happy dogs tearing down our wide beaches against the backdrop of endless waves. Not to see dogs anywhere.

"What're you suggesting?" Dalen asked, and kissed the back of Bren's hand, right on the black skull tattoo. Joey squeezed my knee. It was touching his on the cold floor where we were sitting across from our best friends. Our social bubble.

Bren was quiet for a moment, and I realized I was holding my breath. *Don't forget to breathe,* Joey said on those days we pulled out and paralleled our yoga mats, and he noted that my shoulders were high and tense. The best thing ever was when we were in Savasana and his fingers crawled, crab-like, across the floor to meet mine.

"A beach party," she said, looking into each of our eyes in turn. Holding the gaze. "Like the old days. Let's spread the word."

*

I'm in Vancouver against my parents' wishes. They freaked that I would even *think* of boarding the once-a-week ferry and come to the city to visit Joey, but my passenger application was accepted and there were super strict protocols. I saw an orca on the crossing—that *must* have been a sign. Plus, I had to come: Joey's own family refuses to leave the island until the next vaccine works its way down the line to them. He only has me.

I'm staying in one of the safe pop-up isolation shelters created for hospital visitors, and as public transportation's suspended in the city, I shield, glove, and slip the disposable cape over my slicker, the plastic footwear protectors over my scuffed Blundstones each morning before I walk the fifteen blocks through the wet, rose-lined streets to sit beside Joey's bed at Vancouver General.

At the hospital entrance I remove the plastic from my torso and boots and am given a fresh white set by the shielded hospital guard—sometimes, with all the get-ups we're mandated to wear, it's difficult to distinguish sex. He or she also takes my temperature. Good to go. My GPS app—we're required to use them to aid in contact tracing—is linked to the hospital's via Bluetooth, and then I'm approved.

The intensive care wing is an ocean of sounds. Beeping IV pumps, buzzers, rattle-wheeled carts, cries, angry outbursts, gasping ventilators, intercoms directing someone to do something STAT. It's full capacity. Ominous. A horror show.

I don't know how the medical staff handles all this. It seems procedures and legislation change daily, but what doesn't change is the thick fog of grief that hangs over everything. There's little comfort in the fact that every country in the world is going through the same shit, or far worse. In the hardest hit locations, where citizens are no longer allowed to live in their own homes or go to work, people are corralled into government-controlled camps. Militias roam the streets and shoot to kill. Everything's closing: skies, borders, doors, economies, civilizations.

*

A beach party, in a tidal-pooled cove far from patrolling eyes. We arrived covertly between the Douglas firs and Western red cedars and Arbutus, red-skinned as a heart. Fifty people? Sixty? Didn't matter. We were currents. We hugged. We danced around the beach-wood fire wearing headphones and smelling of smoke. We shared burritos and booze, Molly and marijuana. We knew each other and we didn't. We bled into and out of the shadows while the sea gushed toward us across the shell and kelp-littered beach. Young, alive. Bren was on Dalen's shoulders, mouth-to-bottle, dreadlocks flying.

"Hold my hand," Joey said, and we slithered through the bodies to make love on a moss bed above a shingle beach.

"Listen, it's like a chandelier breaking," I said, as the surf rolled across the littoral stones and shells, then sucked back from the shoreline. In, and out. In, and out. Slowly, slowly.

"The sea has lungs too," he said, and we made love again. It was the first time I'd felt free in two years. Fuck you, restrictions.

*

I'm stronger than my parents. On cull day it was me who leashed Boy, fed him a hamburger and drove him to the incineration site. A hideous day, but I did it. It didn't kill me. It's like life gives you these tests and you think: *This, this is the worst thing that will ever happen to me,* then you realize that *that* nightmare was just training for the next one. And the next one is bigger.

Joey.

Mutations, more mutations. Mother Earth's sucker punch re: overpopulation. So little one can do anymore, but at least I live on the western edge of the world. My town's a chore to get to. There's space.

I pad down the sandy path toward the crashing surf in my booties. All suited up, board a reliable old friend beneath my right arm. Sea air slaps me in the face. The briny scent transports me to the time before.

Offshore winds today. I get hammered. Again, again, again.

*

What will his last sound be? My voice, whispering his name into the soft pink shell of his ear? A nurse ordering me to step behind the curtain as she readjusts his catheter? The saliva and mucous being sucked out of his mouth and breathing tube? The sea pulling back on itself over a shingle beach?

I take a deep breath: in through the nose, out through the mouth. Touch my forehead to Joey's. Sign out. Tomorrow, for sure, I think.

I pass almost no one on the pretty streets as I walk back to the shelter in the grey, late-day light. Rain's at the ready. The roses are discordant. Audaciously pink, yellow, red. I hear a dog barking behind a window, but no, I must be imagining it.

THESE DAYS

Raye Hendrickson

March 20, 2020

The bank door snaps closed behind me   my feet
heavy as I head back to my car.
    I don't know when I will have money
    when I will be back to make another deposit.

I'm shut down. Enforced.
I have to be unavailable.

For the good
of my massage clients   for the good
        of everyone   we all need
to stay away
                from each other.

I dread tonight, going to bed.
How to keep the nugget of fear
            at bay.

March 24, 2020

The article describes it perfectly.

Grief.
The discomfort I'm feeling is grief.

    Loss of normalcy, check mark   no clients
                                        no face-to-face with friends.
    Fear of running out of money, check mark
                                        investments dropping
                                        no income.
    Loss of safety, semi-check mark   we're safe at home
                                        but

being in the presence of others right now is unsafe.
The world feels unsafe.

The article describes "collective grief."
And "anticipatory grief."

I inhabit them.

March 26, 2020

air travel severely curtailed   vehicle traffic greatly diminished
factory productions slowed or shut down

the atmosphere is clearing

Earth is breathing more deeply
taking back her power.

April 9, 2020

Up at 3:30 am   signed up for a CRA account   applied for CERB
      Canada   Emergency   Response   Benefit
            so many of us out of work

people dead   dying   all over the world
    loved ones taking their last breath alone
        selfless people caring for them
            selfless people caring for us

we are trying to stay healthy   stay home
        how can that be enough?

May 11, 2020

My new compulsion
    I track   every day
       the numbers

June 5, 2020

I've made a chart
    lost the paper for last week.

June 6, 2020

The news comes on,
        the numbers.

I don't record them.

February 7, 2021

But every day I listen.

Yesterday
    2,307,000+ dead worldwide

        (!two million plus!)

How can I hold these numbers?

    Each number   a person.

    Each one   a family's grief.

February 8, 2021

Every day
    grateful
        for my partner
        my health
        my work (masked, goggled, aproned)

These days:
no words.

LAKE NOTES

Carla Braidek

The windowpane is cool beneath my palm as flakes so small they are almost pellets sheet from the sky. It will not take long for them to fill the deck in their deliberate way. Already they mask the path and fire pit we used last night.

There were only three of us, awaiting a fourth, gathered very loosely around a welcoming fire not far from the house. Events of the day were quietly shared, including sightings of lynx tracks and the welcome continuation of blue skies and no wind. Casually we poked the fire and wondered if our fourth was going to arrive. This night was an opportunity to say hello while still maintaining recommended distancing. It was also the continuation of a ritual – the burning of the torches. When our words were used up and the waiting was enough, we dipped our tightly rolled cardboards into the blaze of the pit and ambled the path to the lake.

Each torch is fashioned from old tree-planting boxes which are made from wax-coated cardboard, the ideal material for a torch. The roll is secured with a bit of string. A few years ago, my partner took the time to figure this out, and thus began our torch ritual. Torches require night, snow and ideally, not extremely cold temperatures or high winds, though we have gone out in some dubious conditions.

Gripping our torches at the base, we held them upright, so they would not be consumed too quickly. We made our way down the short path, using care as we passed through the treeline of poplar, birch, spruce and tamarack. Arriving on the shore of the lake we trudged out onto its snow-covered surface. Dawson arrived and then we were four. We drifted in slow meanders, partly from the lumpy footing, partly from repeatedly pausing to look at our own and others' torches. None of us strayed too far, perhaps out of laziness, but more likely because of the desire to remain closer during this time of social restraint. There wasn't a lot of conversation, more time was passed admiring the stars, and squinting into torchlight.

And the torches burned. Bright in the velvet sky. We had the perfect night. The sliver moon had not risen so the Milky Way rolled across the heavens. Between us, we could identify four constellations; I managed to find Cassiopeia. We wheeled our arms through the air and the torches flared. Terren tossed his as if to catch it, but then let it drop to the snow, scooped it up and swept it through the air. The torch glowed and blazed. I wrote my name with mine, then stood still and breathed and watched as the others moved and unwittingly wrote brief stories in the night.

On other occasions, we have had as many as eighteen, from grandparents to infants, and the night is boisterous. Everyone who wants a torch gets one. There is much chatter as we prepare, joking back and forth, handing torches about and helping the young ones. A four-year-old runs across the packed snow of the lake in glee, waving her banner. The danger is minimal; if they become afraid, they just drop the torch onto the snow. Everyone knows to keep the distance.

We each go our own way. Some choose to stay in a cluster, or stroll in twos, some lay down, resting their torch beside them in the snow, some dance to unheard music, trailing flames in their wake. We are stars, shifting and finding a place on the expanse of lake. We move, create constellations to find our way. Someone has a sleigh for the littles. It bears discarded toques and scarves. We trudge and sit and lay and hang out on the ice for the hour it takes for the big torches to burn down.

Someone leads the way back as their flame dwindles. When a torch burns short, its bearer perches it on the lake surface and continues the walk home. Torches left behind, glowing in the snow, blaze the trail of where we've been, or perhaps they are the dream of where we will go.

We crouch by the fire pit. Nurse the coals back to a healthy blaze and talk a bit more. Sometimes. Sometimes we are so full of peace, of the immensity of what's happened, that we simply sit, then say goodnight, head to our beds.

Last night, we did not linger by the fire pit. The others paused briefly, appreciated the night and left. There were no heads together to admire stars or snow; there were no arms around shoulders in comfortable comradery. Everyone had carefully stayed in their own space. I pushed still-orange sticks into one another. A small flame leapt up, tenacious. It was time to leave night to itself.

*

Today I walk out, find the remnants of last night's torches. There are only four burn holes in the snow where we placed them. Today's is a solitary walk – no accompanying giggly voices, no quick feet through the snow to locate the markers, identifying who was where.

I mentally note who planted each torch that became today's dirty smudge marks. That recognition seems important, verifying our individual presence in this huge expanse. The shape we created is a small constellation, and it is quickly being obliterated.

A few days ago I walked out on the lake, reveling in the bright sunlight. I moved between the home point and Ant Island, following snowshoe tracks. The lake was open, welcoming – and solidly frozen. There was no wind. It was one of those days you could walk too far and not realize, until too late, that you don't have the energy to return. The world begged me to join her.

I managed to limit myself; paused on the lake to consider my options, and decided to follow another snowshoe track where it skirted between two islands. The firmer surface made for easier walking, but our paths diverged and I continued on my own, breaking trail in ankle-deep snow. Not a difficult task, but slowing me. And I was more than willing to loiter.

The far shore of the lake seemed to keep shifting. Was it the unique angle I approached from that made me consider what I was seeing? There seemed to be small meadows here and there on the shore.

Ah. Mist was rising. A sheer cloud had slipped over the sun. It created ideal conditions for fog. I dropped to my knees and settled back to rest on my lower legs. I wanted this.

The fog grew out of the west, crept along the south shore, along Willy's Point, and ballooned in the north bay. It swelled onto the lake tentatively, careful to be sure it was welcome. Dwindle and surge, it was a tide attempting to fill a space. The haze crept into the south bay and snuck along the east bank. The direction home blurred, tracks thirty feet away faded into mist. Yet behind me was clear. My eyes double-blinked, testing the directions, questioning what to trust. There was immense silence – no bird calls, no vehicles on the road. I did not hear my heart. My knees were not cramped, my feet not cold. There was only the fog, the gift of itself, its offering.

I wanted the wispy vapour to expand and envelope me. I wanted the hug of it; wanted to know its gentleness.

But even the fog kept its distance. The sky nudged the cloud from the sun and the haze receded, much as it had come. Silently, in a sinuous dance, withdrawing more quickly than arriving.

I struggled up, my knees and ankles stiff with immobility. Made my way to the shore, clambered up the path to my yard and into the house. Then I turned around and went out again. There was something out there, and I wanted to bring it home with me. But it had gone. All that remained were the unseen stars in the bright sky. I went in and put water on for tea.

Today, flakes fill paths. The sky is heavier than a shovelful of snow. One mug waits on the table. My fridge is covered with art and photos. And I wonder, what constellations do we create when we travel alone?

STAY IN TOUCH

Glen Sorestad

How often have we spoken
these words with friends or kin
as we bid them a safe trip,

then draw them to us, enclose
them a moment, as if we need
that physical certainty, the other's

heartbeat, on the unthinkable
possibility that this embrace
could be the last?

Perhaps it is our desire to keep
the ones we love safe by saying
stay, when we have already

acknowledged they must leave?
Stay in touch, we implore because
love is every bit as physical

as it is psychological or spiritual.
Do we really need a pandemic
to verify the truth of this for us?

LAST GOODBYE

Belinda Betker

How could I have known?
How could I not have?

I would have taken off
my plastic face shield
hospital mask, and gloves

would have soothed your hands
in mine, asked everything
I'd ever meant to ask

said everything I'd ever meant
to say, would have rested
my bare cheek alongside yours

pressed my ear to your whisper
hugged you without barrier
to say I love you
Mom, love you always.

LEONARD GOES TO FLORIDA

Caitlin McCullam-Arnal

Leonard Owens turned up the radio in his truck. He was heading south, on his way to Dunedin, Florida, to see his daughter Eleanor. He would have sand between his toes for the first time, and maybe even find Rita's shell. His wife, Rita, had hated travelling, but now was Leonard's chance. The radio blared the day's news headlines. In his head he changed the wording slightly: *Local Saskatchewan man with farmer's lung survives one-hundred-vehicle pile-up on Florida Interstate.* "I'm not dead yet," Leonard said out loud.

*

A week earlier, Leonard sat in a plush recliner at his house in Dame, a small town on the outskirts of ranch and farm land. The chair's mechanics buckled as he popped open the footrest. A coffee and cordless phone rested on a floral TV dinner tray. "I ain't dying cuz of a dirty bird," said Leonard. "I'm better than that."

Leonard had farmer's lung.

His doctor said if he caught Covid he would die. At first, in his forties, it was shortness of breath and cough whenever he cleaned a plugged auger, but later in life, the symptoms came up with any kind of dust or wind. Leonard liked to think they moved to town because of Rita's health, but really it was the both of them. They rented out their land and sold off the equipment. Except the Montgomery section, named after the family Leonard bought it from. Leonard would never get any money off that land again, not after his only child, Eleanor, sold it.

"This nonsense government. I'm going to be dead by the time I see a damn needle," Leonard said out loud to his favourite Fox News anchorwoman. "I gots to do something," he said, this time to the glass cupboard above the TV. A university graduation picture of Eleanor sat between a plaque of the Lord's Prayer and Rita's Hummel dolls. The dolls' innocent eyes and cherub cheeks smiled at him.

"Do it," they said.

Instead of the Hummels from her ancestors' Germany, Leonard knew that Rita wanted to collect rare seashells. Rita liked looking for river mussels as a kid, but as an adult became fascinated by cochlear speckled specimens.

She had catalogues delivered to the house but, before she died of cancer two years ago, never made a purchase. She thought it was cheating if she ordered them. "A Florida Junonia only comes after a big storm," Rita had said. It was the ultimate trophy in shell hunting. Bringing home a Junonia shell would be a fine tribute to Rita's memory.

Leonard listened to the news' hourly Covid update. He coughed a little into his coffee mug. Damn lungs. His girl reported on vaccine appointment no-shows in Florida. There were leftover thawed vaccines that had to be administered.

"Well I ain't flying on one of those jumbo jets. Fuckin' planes are cess pools," Leonard said to the dolls.

Then he pushed play on the VCR remote control—Blue Jays 1993 World Series Game—originally seen with his daughter's pigtails blocking the view. Eleanor had to be close to the screen. That was the year Leonard decided to put a section of land in her name. He and Rita couldn't have any more kids. Now Eleanor sent a postcard every spring with a picture of the beach and "Greetings from Dunedin, Florida" in splashy letters. Eleanor wanted to stay in contact. Leonard didn't. They spoke briefly at Rita's funeral.

Unable to concentrate, Leonard grabbed the cordless phone off the metal tray. Once a week he talked to his cousin Lenora. She lived near Niagara Falls. As kids, on the land Leonard eventually inherited, they raised chickens. They sold the eggs and Leonard used the money to buy his first bred heifer. Now, with Rita gone and hard feelings between him and Eleanor, Lenora was the only woman Leonard really talked to.

Today, Lenora wanted to talk helicopters. "These freakin' things used to pass over the house four or five times a day. Now only once or twice. Thank God. They vibrate the windows and walls. Feels like my ears are popping," said Lenora.

"Search and rescue?" asked Leonard.

"Nope. Them snowbirds are hiring 'em to crost the border. Seats three people at a time. Transport trucks drive their camper or car over the border."

"Oh?" said Leonard.

"Yep," she said. "I could never afford to do anything like that."

Then Leonard shifted in his chair. "I was thinking of taking a trip south," he said. He couldn't afford to either, since he made a large donation to the Dame Hall for a new boiler, but he was used to an overdraft on his account.

"Oh?" said Lenora. "To see her?"

"I'm having a hard time," said Leonard, ignoring her question. "Lenora, I thinks I'm gonna die."

"Bud, you gots time. My arthritis has been acting up more," said Lenora. "But you think *travellin'* is the answer?" she asked.

Leonard ignored this question too. "Yup. Maybe you could find me a ticket for one of them things."

"Maybe," said Lenora.

After he hung up, he looked at the dolls.

"I'm doing it," he said back to them.

*

Leonard checked into his room at the Stay-Away Inn, a turquoise-trimmed motel on the outskirts of Tallahassee. He had driven to Florida in two days. Coming into the city, he'd rolled down the window of his truck and waited for the warm breeze to hit his face, but it was cold—even hurt his lungs. Actually, the temperature in Tallahassee wasn't that much different from Niagara Falls.

He wasn't staying near the pharmacy. Lenora had picked his destinations. Then Leonard put them into his GPS. "That Lenora coulda done better coordinating things," he said out loud, as he turned on the TV. The news reported freezing temperatures for northern Florida, a system from Canada. After he got out of his bath, he would call the pharmacy, and book his vaccine. Then he thought of Rita. He would find out where the beach was too.

*

"Evening," answered a young woman.

"I need a vaccine," said Leonard, towel in hand. He barely cleaned himself in the motel's soap-holder-sized bathtub. Now the hand towel wasn't doing the trick either.

"Okay," she responded. "Well, sir, let me get you on a list. See where we're at for bookings. Last I looked it would be in two weeks," she said.

"What? I ain't got that time," Leonard thought about his negative bank account and failing lungs. "Don't you got a whole bunch on hand?"

"Yeah, no," laughed the woman. "There's others waiting. Then you have to wait a couple weeks for the second shot. Don't you know?"

He didn't. "Well, what am I supposed to do?" he asked.

"I don't know. I just make the lists," said the woman.

Leonard changed his tactic. "What about the closest beach?"

"Yeah, no, sir," she laughed. "There's no beaches in Tallahassee. Closest city with beaches is Jacksonville, and it's a three-hour drive. All we got is alligators and swamp. Used to have college football before the virus."

Leonard hung up.

*

On a Monday, Leonard locked his front door in Dame and thought about putting a note in the mailbox for Marv the mailman. "Na. It'll be fine," Leonard said to the metal railing leading down the steps. He would be back before anyone noticed he was gone. He didn't tell a soul where he was going, not even Eleanor, his daughter, and she was *in* Florida. She was a sports physical therapist for the Blue Jays. She had written to him in February to say they were still going to Dunedin for spring training, despite Covid. Every year she invited Leonard to come. It was an opportunity for him to meet the players. During the regular season—no special visits. Leonard always never responded.

An hour outside of Regina, Leonard got on the TransCanada. At first, the drive was just like home—flat as a pancake. Then, outside of Winnipeg, the road opened up to three eastbound lanes. Traffic got heavier. Leonard felt like he might shit his pants. To calm himself, he repeated, "anything east of Winnipeg exists because of the west. Anything east of Winnipeg exists because of the west."

"*Don't you forget that, Leonard,*" his dad had always warned.

"I won't," said Leonard out loud to a small sports car whizzing by on his outside lane.

Leonard's steering wheel sweated all through Northern Ontario. Still, he preferred the threat of trees to traffic. At a gas station in Kapuskasing, a man said, "bonjour." It sounded like a swear word to Leonard. His dad always said: "*Only English, Leonard. That's all you gots to speak, you hear,*" something he failed to pass onto his daughter Eleanor. She got an entrance scholarship to a bilingual university in Ottawa. "*Sheesh,*" his dad used to always say.

When Leonard reached Toronto on Wednesday his hips hurt from sleeping in the backseat of his truck. His blue eyes were coated insulation pink. Around suppertime, the signs to Niagara Falls had reached ten kilometres. Leonard took the exit for Lenora's street, happy to hear the hum of slow-moving vehicles again. Pulling into Lenora's driveway, Leonard saw her face through the paisley curtains of her bungalow's south-facing bay window. She was holding her phone. It was the first time seeing her outside of Saskatchewan. He turned off his engine. Then he heard his phone ring.

"Hey! You made it!" Lenora said, waving out the window.

"Course I did," said Leonard into his phone. He waved back.

"Got some bad news," said Lenora.

"What's that?" Leonard asked and unclipped his seatbelt.

"The roast beef's in the oven," said Lenora.

That's all Leonard wanted to hear.

"Leonard… ya can't come in."

"What?" The seat belt crept up his plaid shirt.

"The neighbours." She turned away from the window now.

"And?" Leonard said. He stopped himself from opening the truck door.

"You gots to go."

"It's my Saskatchewan plates, ain't it?" asked Leonard.

"I'll gets a fine. Don't you see I called? Went to voicemail." Lenora turned to face the glass again. She rubbed her left eye. "This lockdown. I can't."

"You're going to leave me on the doorstop?" Leonard said.

"Guess so." She began to tear up.

Looking out his truck window, ignoring Lenora now, Leonard saw a woman coming towards him, walking a dog. His truck was blocking the sidewalk so she had to go around. He didn't know if she smiled behind her mask, but she certainly didn't return Leonard's wave. "Unfriendly Eastern buggers," Leonard said.

*

Leonard slept in the backseat of his truck in the parking lot of the Trans America Helicopter Company, outside Niagara Falls, an hour after leaving his cousin's. With roast beef sandwiches and potato salad in his belly, a wee bit of his family, he dreamed about the beach. Leonard's family was all together looking for shells. Eleanor hadn't sold the land. She kept it like she was supposed to, got married, and farmed it with her husband, instead of selling it to the neighbours to pay for school. In and out of dream state, Leonard wasn't paying for that nonsense.

In the morning, slightly disoriented, but excited, Leonard walked into an airport for the first time. He expected it to be crowded with people from other countries. Instead, it looked like a motel lobby. An older woman sat at a desk. She looked like she could be from Saskatoon.

"Your name?" she asked.

Leonard's mouth got dry, like he was eating paper. He was afraid of flying. "Leonard Owens," he squeaked.

"Mr. Owens, I have you leaving in half an hour for Buffalo, New York. Here's your ticket. Please wait." She pointed to a row of plastic chairs. "We'll call you up. And your keys?"

He had to remind himself, he was going to get the vaccine, an attempt to save himself.

"Yes'm," said Leonard.

"Transport will be here in fifteen minutes. Do you have your valuables out of the vehicle?" It just struck him that someone else would be driving his truck. His dad always taught him never to let a stranger drive their vehicles, but eventually, he had to hand over the keys.

*

On Sunday morning, the day after he arrived, Leonard checked out of the motel in Tallahassee. He had on a dirty shirt and pants. He packed light thinking Lenora would've done his laundry. His head hung low, as he told the young woman at the desk, "I couldn't get the vaccine. Now I'm headed home."

She took her hands off the keyboard of her computer. "I'm sorry to hear that, Sir, but if it makes you feel any better, I still haven't gotten mine. Now, do you want to use the credit card on file?" she asked.

"Ah, yes'm," said Leonard. He looked around the motel lobby. It had been a trip of disappointment for him—no vaccine, no shell. He couldn't afford to stay any longer either. There was only so much overdraft his bank account could handle before he got a phone call.

"Good thing you're setting out. If this weather keeps up we will be without power. Come to think of it, I better call my boyfriend to pick up batteries for our flashlights. Now, you come back anytime, you hear? Sorry I can't offer you any coffee." She put up her hands in defeat. "Covid rules," she said.

Outside Leonard watched sleet pelt the palm trees next to the motel's outdoor pool. A group of giggling students raised the hoods of their spring jackets and snapped pictures of the weather as they too walked to their vehicles. Leonard copied them and took out his phone. He didn't know where Dunedin was but knew it was in Florida.

She picked up after the first ring, "Hey Dad."

He knew he had to do *something*. He wasn't going into the grave without trying.

"Eleanor, why did you sell the land? Why aren't you married?"

*

His wipers brushed slush off his windshield. With his new all-season tires, he wasn't worried about icy roads. As he drove away from the Stay-Away Inn, he found the interstate easily. He pushed on the gas and merged north, towards home. The conversation with Eleanor hadn't gone well. Neither one was budging. In the rearview mirror, he saw a blue car, low to the ground. It wasn't following close, but Leonard could see it clearly. She kept telling him she had a good job, what more could he ask for? The sleet was falling heavy now and his windshield wipers creaked. He wanted her married, to come back home. The next time he looked up the blue car was sliding left, then right.

"Holy shit," Leonard said out loud. He knew not to brake, but reduce his speed. When he looked up again he heard a pop and squealing tires. Then, like out of a Peter Fonda movie, the car behind him spun out, flipped, and landed on its top in the middle of the freeway.

"Holy fuck," said Leonard. He turned around and took his foot off the gas completely, tasted his morning waffles in the back of his throat. He thought about the message that was being sent to him.

HEAD SOUTH, LEONARD!

He pulled over, put on his four way flashers. Thought about taking out his phone to dial 911, but instead, checked his mirror and started driving again. He took the next exit and swallowed his pride. As the compass on his rearview mirror changed from "N" to "S", he wasn't dead yet, and neither was his trip.

IF YOU WERE HERE

Joan Crate

It's April, but it's not Spring.
The trees hunch against endless winter
and snow scurries like flies through a corpse.

I am tired of missing you, fed up
with waiting for you to emerge
from the soggy corners of dream, exhausted
by nightmares of an assassin bursting
through the front door, horrified
by my porous bones and thin skin, how easily
I break.

If you were here, we would find this isolation
an extravagance, lie down in new grass
poking through snow in the backyard and grow
sheaves of summer. If you were here,
your body would be turning mine to fireflies
on a lick of warm breeze.

I would plant a tree for you, a maple
with scarlet leaves or the giant Lebanese cedar
your brother stood under a month
before he was blown up.

We would stack daylight to burn
when we're dark but can't sleep,
when we want to talk of grandchildren
and forever, plan a trip to water and fossils,
have a bath for hours.

If you were here, I would take you
for granted, snipe impatient
at your stale jokes, grow friendly
when you stroke me like a fur coat.

I'd hold you like the incoming tide,
lick the salt from your skin and make you
listen while I psychoanalyse
every relationship I've ever had
except ours.

I'd place it in a box with the children's teeth
and umbilical cords, your favourite lingerie
of mine, the card you gave me our first Christmas
together, your hunger, your bicycle,
your last will and testament
unsigned.

I wouldn't have been pulled inside
out, lungs hung like withered balloons
from splintered ribs, heart a chunk of raw meat
decaying. I wouldn't miss you hungrily,
achingly, miserably, philosophically,

wouldn't have to write this fucking poem
if you'd just come home.

LOSING ELLIS

Jill Robinson

Note: Names have been changed.

I'd just arrived on Galiano Island after visiting my son in Victoria, and I intended to spend three or four nights at the cabin before heading back home to Banff. First thing, even before I unpacked the car, I hiked up the hill to turn on the solar panel and the water. I was expecting the cistern to be full from last autumn, but it wasn't: it was *empty* except for maybe three inches of water. What gives? I thought. I looked more closely and saw that the black pvc pipe that carries the water from the well to the cistern was broken, and that's how all the water had drained out. Shit. No water. Which was a big disappointment because we'd sunk a big whack of dough into finishing the cabin so that one of us could come out here for a month or two even through winter. Last summer was the first time everything was up and running tickety boo and I must say it had been glorious. Electricity! Hot and cold running water! Imagine!

Now, it was March, and the time of the rapid implementation of Covid-19 regulations, and suddenly travel was discouraged. I was fearful about being out in the open with my Alberta plates even if I drove right through, and so I decided I'd stay on Galiano as long as necessary. Why not? There were worse places to be than on a small island surrounded by sea, in a cabin in the forest up a grassy driveway 300 metres from the nearest neighbour. I didn't have to see anyone, didn't have to touch anything anyone might have touched, didn't have to breathe the same air as anyone except my dog. Ringo. Now, feeling intrepid, I put on disposable surgical gloves and filled water jugs at the neighbour's, and I emailed our friend Ellis about helping me fix the cistern. Sure, he responded promptly. Sure, he'd help me.

Good old Ellis. The cistern wasn't exactly his area of expertise: he was first and foremost a surveyor. But his range of interests was wide and he enjoyed solving problems, and he was one of those people who are just good at fixing things. Whenever I was at the cabin on my own, I regularly plied him with ice cream and crib games so he'd never abandon me. He was on his own: he'd lost his wife to anger and then death, several years ago now.

He came over and we drank tea together at the picnic table near the cabin. He sat down at one end of the picnic table on one side and folded his long legs under it, and I sat at the other. As I'd asked, he brought cookies. But instead of my favourites, those round chocolate-covered marshmallow and biscuit ones with a layer of strawberry jam, or even chocolate chip, or shortbread, he brought Mr. Christie's Social Tea Biscuits. "Thanks," I said, frowning as I took the package of ultra plain rectangular cookies. "I think." Ellis laughed as he held out the cup he'd brought, and I poured the tea.

"Good to see you," I said.

"You too," he said.

"But I think you're looking a bit too thin."

"Not enough ice cream. How've you been?"

Ringo was busy sniffing around Ellis's van looking for Baron, Ellis's dog, and whining with incredulous disbelief. Where was he? For the first time ever, Ellis had left his dog at home, and Ringo was miffed. He looked balefully at me: I'd told him that Baron was coming. I myself didn't miss Baron, though I'd never have said that. Baron is an unkempt, smelly, hairy ill-mannered, ocean-stink, unbathed Airedale who heedlessly runs into me, jumps up and tries to slobber, pant and clamber through the van window and I just don't like him. However, that's not how Ellis felt. Or Ringo.

"How are things with Loren?" Ellis asked. "Or should I ask?" He gave a half laugh.

"Okay, I guess," I said. "He's moved back to Saskatoon."

"Weren't you done with Saskatoon?"

"That's where the new woman is."

"New woman, eh?"

"Yessir."

He shook his head. "I can't get my head around that."

"Me neither. Ha ha."

"I mean, I can't imagine a man leaving a woman like you."

"Oh Ellis!" I said. A sunbeam of gratitude lit up and warmed me from inside and lifted my heart. "Just what I needed to hear. You are the best!"

And I reached over to lay my hand on his but remembered Covid and pulled back. It was the end of March, and neither of us had got the hang of all things Covid yet, like everyone on the planet, just flung into quarantine, and though Ellis and I made an attempt, we still screwed up. We were good about the cups, and the cookies – I slid them out of the package onto a plate and we were careful to take the ones we touched – but when I wanted to show him a picture of the cistern problem I handed my phone to him as a person normally would do, and he took it from me as a person normally would do, and looked at the picture and handed the phone back to me, and in that moment our eyes met in sudden and mutual recognition of what we'd just done. I felt panic rising. I ran inside for the hand sanitizer. I'd made it just that morning. Aloe vera and rubbing alcohol.

*

If it rains, it pours. That night Ringo, after chasing a deer, returned panting heavily with delight from exertion, and with a nasty cut on his foreleg. Shit.

I had to take him over to the vet on Mayne Island the next day and we missed the ferry back, but thankfully my camping gear was still in the trunk so it was no big deal for us to stay overnight and come back to Galiano the following day. I called Ellis from the ferry line-up. He'd fixed the cistern, he said. His helper, Bobby, had been along as well. "Thanks so much," I said. "You're wonderful!"

"Well, I don't know about that," he said.

He sounded a bit low-key.

"What's wrong?"

"Oh, I went to bed early last night, and I've been there all day. My tummy's upset."

I smiled to myself—the way he referred to it as his tummy.

"It was something I ate," he said. "Golden beets gratin. They were so good I ate too many."

"Yikes," I said, and then the ferry started to load and I had to say goodbye. "Get better," I said. "Talk soon." But I thought about Covid, and hoped he didn't have it and felt a rush of fear that if he had Covid then I might too, because we'd both touched my phone like that. "Please," I said to my stricken face in the rear-view mirror. "Please don't let me have Covid. Please." Back at the cabin, I gave Ringo a pain-killer, checked the bandage on his wound, invited him up on the bed and we napped long and deep together, spooning.

The next day, the sun broke through for a couple of hours, and around three I climbed the hill to the cistern and had a look. I stopped to catch my breath part way up and imagined how hard it must have been for Ellis with his bad knees and heart condition. That man was not in good shape, and this hill could do anyone in. It was sure nice of him to help me. He always did.

The pipe was hooked back up again and sealed tight. I stood on the wooden platform and unscrewed the black stopper and peered into the cistern. Maybe seven inches of water. Yes! Things were getting better. I dumped in a bit of bleach to take care of the grunge and went back down to the cabin. Soon. Soon I could fill the hot water tank and turn it on and at least part of life would be good again.

It was going to be strange getting used to Loren's not puttering around absorbed in his projects and activities. We'd established a rhythm over the years; I'd liked how we worked around each other, each in our own orbit, and overlapped at meals, the beach, the crib board, or with the friends we'd made on the island, including Ellis. I liked watching Loren from my writing porch as he got his power tools out of the shipping container and set to work building or fixing. Or when he loaded his kayak on the roof of his car, gathered his life jacket, paddles, waterproof pouch, and headed for the boat launch at Montague Harbour. More stuff if it was an overnight trip. And then his arrival back home again, and my asking if he needed a hand unloading the kayak and the rest of the gear. We were together and apart in a way that worked. Just for me, it turned out. There would be no more of that.

I couldn't reach Ellis by email or by phone. I should have gone over to check on him but I was worried about Covid. When he finally answered the phone, he sounded even lower, and he said he felt he'd had some kind of a blockage, he'd had a horrendous stomach ache like he'd never in his life had before. And then, he said, all of a sudden in the middle of the night WHOOSH came torrents of diarrhoea so bad he couldn't get to the bathroom. (At this point, I didn't want to hear a fricking word, held the phone away from my ear and went *Ay Ay Ay* though I heard it anyway.) Finally there was a pause.

Barely able to speak, I said, "I have to go."

And he said, "I'm going back to sleep."

"Sweet dreams," I said. "Call 911 if you get any worse. I'm serious."

*

Over the next couple of days I settled into my new old familiar life on the property. I dragged the fireplace grate out from under the cabin and filled it with the flat of flame-coloured marigolds I'd brought over. I filled and hung the bird feeders. I started clipping the overgrown salal on my trails, watering and weeding my pathetic raised bed of rosemary, mint, and oregano. I fertilized the two remaining rose bushes in the stone corner bed Loren had made for them.

Around suppertime on Wednesday, Ellis's neighbour called to tell me that on Tuesday the paramedics had entered Ellis's house in Covid gear and rushed him to the boat dock in an ambulance; from there he had travelled by float plane to the closest major hospital, where in the midst of testing he had collapsed and died.

I didn't know what to do when I got the call; "Thank you," I said, and the call ended, and then I was frozen standing there in the cabin with Ringo looking at me. Wondering. "Oh, no!" I whispered. "Ellis is dead." Ringo's tail wagged slightly: what was I saying?

Oh, no! The world was different, shifted in that second. Dead! The circles each of us has around us. Ellis, I thought. Oh Ellis. And then I thought again of myself and grew afraid. "Please," I said again. "Please don't let him have had Covid."

I called Loren. I know. But I did. He's the only person in the world who knows Ellis without my having to explain everything. This, I thought as I called, is an example of what will happen more often, the cumbersome task of having to establish context and history and precedent before explaining anything to someone new, whereas after so many years with the two of us entwining history the other of us just understood what we meant by many things, people, situations. "Call me," I managed to croak to his voicemail. And lo and behold, he did.

I could barely talk – have you ever been so stressed your throat constricts and you make a heaving sound like a backwards groan while you're trying to suck enough air inward while also trying to breathe, and trying to speak? That's what happened. But it got easier, and I told him what I knew, except that I was afraid of having Covid. And I thought after the call ended that he hadn't offered me any comfort. Had I expected some? *How are you doing? Are you okay?* Foolish woman. Get a grip and lower your expectations. He's not the man you thought he was. *Goodness,* was all he said, over and over, when I told him about Ellis. *Goodness. Goodness.*

*

The next day, Ringo and I walked down to Ellis's house, which looked just the same but of course wasn't because he wasn't inside anymore. Through that very door, I thought, they took him, the door now closed so innocently with its curtain drawn. I stuck a note with my name and phone number in the frame for whoever comes to take care of things; I offered my help. I didn't try the door and the windows were too dirty to see through and anyway the sun was wrong. Turning away I thought how somebody was going to have one hell of a job cleaning out his house. He had so much stuff, and the whole place had perpetually needed a major clean. The smell would be just horrible in there now. Dirty dog and diarrhoea. I wondered again about Covid. How many days before it was safe to go inside? And then I wondered about Baron—where was the dog? Not there.

Back at the cabin, I climb the hill behind the cabin up to the wellhead. The cistern is full to the brim with clean, cold water from six hundred feet down. I open the valves and the water gushes down the hill through the pipe and into the underworld of the cabin. I go down and crawl on my belly on plywood scraps and open the valves, and I hear the water gush inside to the toilet, the hot water tank, the shower, the sink. And then from inside the cabin I hear the ping of my email, and I go inside. Ellis's neighbour says Ellis did not die of Covid. He had a heart attack. Relief floods through me; I haven't realized how tense I've been. I turn on the tap, fill a tall glass of cold water, quench my deep thirst.

I HOPE: A LOVE NOTE FROM GRANDMA

Janet Hainstock

I hope when you look out your window tonight, you see the same moon I am looking at too.

I hope when you remember a lullaby I have sung, you know I am remembering to sing it too.

I hope when you pray for me before you go to sleep, you know I am praying for you too.

I hope when you dream, you see my face and you know when I dream I am seeing your face too.

I hope when you wake up and put on your favourite blue apron, you know I am putting on my apron that is just like it too.

I hope when you and your mom make pancakes for breakfast, you know I am making pancakes just like them too.

I hope when you have licked all the syrup off your plate, you know I am licking the syrup off my plate too.

I hope when you play in your yard today, you know I wish I was there playing with you too.

So until we can meet at the swings to play, I hope you know I will always love you.

SORROWFUL SKY

Rita Bouvier

I reach out into the mysterious depth of the unknown
now on this n^{th} day of self-isolation   grieving

a strong gust of spring wind promises to lift my spirit
in the measure of clouds swirling across a fearless blue sky

white-headed gulls soar high overhead
a choreography of wings   each the span of a butterfly's wing

from this vantage point I touch sky   holding her white ribbons
of cloud in my hands   an invocation for the sick and the dying.

WHERE THE NEED IS GREATEST

Alison Lohans

Meg slumped into the hammock, lifting her feet and not caring that the chains screeched against the frame overhead. There was no need to look up to the robin singing nearby. For once, the rundown rental house next door was mercifully quiet, apart from occasional coughing. A mosquito whined about her right cheek. She slapped it, then wiped the smear of insect parts off her hand. A squirrel ran along the fence. Until recently, Henri, her elderly Bichon-cross, would've gone out of his mind barking at this intruder. Now he lay snoozing on the shady grass, though an ear twitched.

Jim. Her heart wrenched. This September was wrapped in grey, despite its bright sunshine and clear air, with vibrant greens and flowers blooming into the cusp of autumn. In May, Jim had gone to help out where the need was greatest. *And he never came back…* Her over-tired body ached from far too little sleep during the past months, and she was quite sure their dog was grieving too.

Under lockdown conditions there was no one to be with now that she was laid off, no opportunity for the blessing of human touch, even by accident. All her friends were tied up with their families, in their own bubbles. Her sister Nan was in far-away Arizona, tending to her husband with his own set of ailments. Sometimes people phoned, messaged on Facebook and the like, even left things in her mailbox. But nobody knew how to address her bereavement – particularly since Jim had left her to fend for herself in Regina, while he used his nursing skills where there was dire need. It was truly selfless, and admirable…but *he* wasn't supposed to get sick, too!

Collective trauma… The term came up often during her grief counselling. By phone, of course.

In her lap, her phone remained silent.

A different squeak caught her attention. She sat up in the hammock, setting the frame jiggling. The hinges of the back gate shouldn't be moving, should be dormant, like most everything else. Henri noticed too, rousing from his long nap with a subdued *"Wuff."* The dog looked at her with his soulful brown eyes, then trotted over to the gate.

A little girl crept in, the girl from next door. Likely eight or so, her nose was crusted with dried snot and tangled hair spilled across a dirty, tight-fitting t-shirt. There were bruises – dark fingerprints wrapped around one upper arm, and a mottled patch marred her left cheekbone.

Meg's breath caught in her throat as Henri, barking, ran straight to the little girl's feet.

"Puppy!" the child exclaimed, stooping to pet him. Then, squinting, she looked around the yard. Defiant dark eyes met Meg's. With a kick, she shoved Henri aside, who'd jumped up in greeting.

"Hey!" Meg said. "Don't hurt my dog!" Not, *what are you doing here?* Or, *who hurt you?*

After another ferocious look, the little girl seemed to weigh something in her mind. Then she raced across the yard. And disappeared through Meg's back door.

"Hey!" Meg shoved her phone into her shorts pocket and lurched to her feet. Reflexively, she reached down to comfort a confused Henri, who'd run to her side after the kick. A dried weed-head dangled from the pale wool on one ear; she carefully plucked it out, then ran up the back steps. *What was that child doing, in* her *house?*

In the kitchen, she was greeted by a gaping refrigerator door that revealed muddled contents. Milk carton leaning precariously on its shelf, yellow mustard bottle already on the floor, yawning drawers rifled through with clear plastic bags hanging over their sides.

"Hey!" she yelled again – and was answered only by departing thuds of small feet, followed by the slam of the front door. As she stood there, frozen with indecision, the milk carton leaned further and cartwheeled to the floor, trailing a white stream. Henri enthusiastically began lapping at the growing puddle.

Swearing, Meg retrieved the carton and put it back in the refrigerator. The new loaf of multigrain rye was missing, as were two packages of cold cuts and her big hunk of cheddar. She sank down to sit on the floor, weeping, stroking her dog, who continued to enjoy the unexpected cool treat. She'd clean up the mess later.

*

Even after the second sleeping pill, it was apparent that there was little likelihood of sleep that night. The evil taste of zopiclone in the back of her mouth taunted her; it was always this way when the medication failed to do its job. The upstairs room was too hot despite its open window, and the oscillating fan swiveled in unhelpful directions. Meg freed herself from the tangle of sheets and got up to rotate the base of the fan so the moving air covered a friendlier trajectory. On her bed, Henri snored gently.

Next door, the usual tumult blasted from the rental house. Incessant music with pulsing, penetrating bass that reverbed in her viscera. Raised voices, laughter, swearing, the clanking of bottles, all travelled on the night air. A heated argument developed, accompanied by the sound of repeated slaps, screams, things crashing. And loud coughing.

Meg went to the window. With hands clapped over her ears, she screamed out through the screen, *"Stop it, for God's sake!"* If anyone heard, there was no sign; the barrage of noise continued.

The little girl lived there. People – at least *somebody* – hit her, perhaps often. She was obviously famished, to have raided the fridge. Was she terrified? Or, by now, passively numb?

Call the police? Likely not the best idea; living next door as she did, made her an easy target for revenge. In the morning she'd phone Social Services; at the very least they ought to step in to help the little girl.

And what about Covid? She shivered despite the heat, thinking of Jim – how he'd fallen ill, with almost no means of communicating across the distance; how he'd died up north...*alone.* New tears leaked out as her midriff once again convulsed at this unfathomable loss. She collapsed onto the bed – *now only* her *bed* – drawing Henri's warm, unresisting self against her. Her fingers found some comfort, tracing through his soft fur. His tongue flicked out and glanced against her wet cheek.

*

The next day seemed blacker, despite sunlight flooding through windows. Everything was heavy and hurt, and now her throat rasped as well – predictable, after so many nights with too-little sleep. Meg dutifully swallowed a Cold FX and a handful of Vitamin C, nearly choking as the large tablets caught on the back of her tongue. It would be simplest to just get sick, *really* sick, and...

With the kettle already on, she dumped the last of her coffee beans into the grinder, adding a portion of instant so her morning brew would have more of a kick than old dishwater. Pressing her thumb to the switch, she noticed Henri waiting, more impatiently than usual, at the back door for his morning pee. As the boiling water dripped through the blend in the filter, she let her dog out.

An eruption of barking followed. No squirrels roamed the fence tops, nor any of the branches she could see – though an annoyed robin squawked as he took refuge in the crab-apple tree, with its bright red fruit and leaves showing their first tinges of yellow. Gripping the edges of the twin sinks, Meg leaned forward to peer further out the window. At this interference, her coffee and filter tipped, spilling their precious contents straight toward the drain. Meg swore and grabbed, righting it before it had *all* disappeared, earning herself a streak of scalding liquid and grounds across her wrist. By the time she'd wiped it off, Henri was pawing at the back door.

The day passed in a grim haze. Remembering the little neighbour girl, she dutifully found the number for Social Services and, since it was *not* an emergency that warranted calling 9-1-1, she waited on Hold, having been assured that her call was important to them but there would be longer-than-usual delays due to Covid-19. Finally she hung up without success, and collapsed on the couch.

Her phone dinged with a text from her sister Nan in faraway Arizona. *So sorry I've been out of touch,* it read. *David's @ cardiologist rt now & I'm waiting in car, can't go inside. How ARE you??? Love you & big hugs, n*

Meg's eyes blurred, because that's what they *did,* these past couple of months. How could she possibly respond with her own issues, when her brother-in-law was so seriously ill?

Henri's sharp, urgent yapping resolved that particular dilemma. Again he bark-danced his way toward the back door. Looking through the screen, she saw a set of small, pale buttocks squatting near the fence. Dizziness swept through her. *Now what…?!* Probably best not to go out and startle the child, mid-defecation….

Overwhelmed, she leaned against the door frame. *Breathe!* commanded the all-knowing voice of her therapist, Andrea. Shaking, eyes squeezed shut, she obeyed, safely supported by the wall. When she next looked, there was no sign of the intruder. Ripping the last sheet of paper towel from the roll, she had to race Henri to get to the turd, even had to gently but firmly push him aside. It was still warm as her hand-with-towel gingerly wrapped around it. *If she and Jim had only been able to have kids…* Again she convulsed in tears, and dropped to her knees on the warm grass. Which needed mowing. *Again.* Already… *Go for a walk,* Andrea's voice interrupted. *It's a gorgeous day, and it would be good for you to have a change of scenery.*

Why was her therapist talking to her like this? But it was too obvious. She was beyond exhausted, and over-wrought. When a person went too long without sleep, they'd begin hallucinating, making up for missed REM sleep. Meg forced herself to her feet. Better to have Andrea talking in her head, saying useful things, than a lot of other people. She tossed the paper-towel-with-turd into the garbage bin, where it landed with a hollow *thud.* And then noticed Henri, also squatting by the still-blooming rosebush. Retrieving the shovel from its usual place leaning against the garage, she scooped up this latest prize. Though it was against the law, this second offering followed its predecessor, unwrapped.

"C'mon, Henri," she said. "Let's go for a walk."

Immediately her sweet Bichon-cross was dancing about her feet, eyes alit. Inside, she grabbed his leash, then one of her masks, which she tucked in her pocket. Her phone, and wallet-with-keys-attached. Then, to Henri's great confusion, she stalled. Selected an apple and a banana from the fruit bowl, a couple of juice boxes, a handful of carrots, and a half-full box of crackers. After all, eating was quite irrelevant now, and her once-tight clothes hung more easily about her. She set the stash on an old plastic plate, which she placed just outside the back door, and led a leashed-and-puzzled Henri past it, just out of reach.

And this time it was Jim's voice: *Be careful, Meggie.* Her throat clamped around devastated tears, fighting back unholy sounds that longed to escape. At her side, Henri whimpered and huddled against her.

Emerging from the back lane, they went several blocks, stopping at every single tree, every streetlight post, and other random dog targets. The day didn't change colour.

When they returned, the food was no longer by the back door. The plate lay rakishly at the base of the bottom step; a banana peel was in mid-lawn, and the cracker box *and* juice boxes were near the hammock. Where the little girl was curled up, sound asleep. A long scratch raked along her forearm. And another bruise, a fresh one, blackened one eye.

"*Oh my God!*" Unclipping Henri's leash, Meg chewed her bottom lip.

Meggie, be careful! Jim's voice, again.

Strength roared in, a torrential gust of it. "*Damn you, James Merrick!*" The staggering fury left her shaking. "*Damn you, DAMN YOU!*" She grabbed the abandoned plate and hurled it over the fence. "You had to go and leave me. To help *other* people. Why'd you have to *die,* damn you?"

The little girl sat up in the swaying hammock – while Henri snuffled around, found the apple core, and settled down to enjoy it.

"Don't hit me!" Her voice was high and shrill. The child rocked to her feet, obviously terrified. She wore the same tight, filthy t-shirt as yesterday, now with a dark rust-coloured splotch – *blood?* – near the hem. As before, snot crusted her lower face, today smeared across one cheek as well. When she took a step toward the back gate, she swayed.

Meg knelt beside her. "Are you all right, sweetheart?" A huge determination centred her. Jim had gone to help where the need was greatest, far away. But here was another huge need, in her own backyard.

"Don't hurt me!" the little girl whimpered. She stumbled, and fell.

Meggie…! Again, Jim's voice.

Meg reached for the child, lifted her. She was burning with fever.

Kids are superspreaders.

The warning sizzled through her. Even so, she held the little girl, supporting her weight against her breast and shoulder. "You're safe with me," she said, brushing tangled hair off the much-too-hot forehead. In the crab-apple tree, a single yellow leaf fluttered down to the grass.

Henri looked up at her then, straight at her, with his soulful brown eyes. Loving eyes; trusting eyes. He did not look away.

Something inside her froze. Her pulse thudded in her ears.

Still cradling the sick child, Meg sat on the warm boards of the back steps.

And phoned the police. Henri trotted over and nestled close against her thigh. As Meg waited on Hold, with the little girl's head resting on her shoulder, her free hand stroked Henri's comforting small self. Her fingers feathered through his soft, glistening fur. Henri sighed and relaxed.

When the call ended, she pulled her mask from her pocket.

NOT TODAY

Karen Nye

Not today, corona. NOT TODAY. You woke me again imagining
headaches, the world locked down imagining
the worst. My poet friends foiled you. We've zoomed you
to submission
            at least for this half hour
            together closer
            with our words.
You don't get to steal those. Our hugs, yes.
Our creations, our hearts, our ever-loving
of this world you are trying hard to destroy – NO.
            Laptop picnic table poetry
            eight brave voices, one encouraging
            mentor. The result uprooted
            plants, the fall
            cleanup, two poems, a heart
            lighter.
Not today, corona. You can not steal
the words, the sunlight, the chirping
breeze, the red leaves, this autumn
air so free of you.

POST PANDEMIC PLANS

Jayne Melville Whyte

I don't want to go back to normal.

I want a world with everyone
sustained by basic income,
enough for rent and groceries.
A world where everyone has a home,
safety, comfort, and clean drinking water.
A world where securities mean friendships,
not hoarded paper – money or toilet tissue.

I want clean air and water
with fulfilling employment
in sustainable communities,
respecting earth and every living being.

I want choices to craft and appreciate
creative vision industries:
art, music, writing, dance,
caring and sharing,
drawing on our love and skills,
when we see a need to serve.

I want a world where education
counts as an investment, not an expense.
Where preventing trauma,
treating addiction and mental illness
supports healthier individuals and society
in spaces where we learn and grow.

I want a world offering these measures
as vaccines to reduce the costs
of jails and human suffering.
I want increased taxes to keep the change.

I don't want the world to go back to normal
as the Covid pandemic wanes.
I want the world to move forward
to something better.

REMEMBRANCE DAY

Tracy Stevens

It was a damned sad Remembrance Day when they finally hauled her body away. There was no mistaking it this time. There was not an ambulance with paramedics or a large, loud engine truck with firefighters masked and gowned but who never unfurled their hoses no matter how many times they arrived, nor what time they arrived. This time it was after the midnight hour, in the dead quiet of the early morning, on the melancholy day set aside for our national mourning.

No emergency vehicles arrived this time. Only police vehicles of all sizes and shapes from sedans to SUVs were parked on our street – a small, quiet bay that opens onto a green space and is within walking distance of two elementary schools, a church and a pedestrian walkway. But the most conspicuous vehicle was the ominous large, sleek, shiny black suburban vehicle.

And then her children arrived in their vehicles, one at a time, some with their partners, the eldest alone. Thankfully, her little girl and her grandbaby were not present. Her kids parked where they could as the police vehicles took up the limited street parking, given the big suburban was backed into the driveway's narrow space. The four ran toward the house they had called home for a few years until this summer when their mother's illness seemed to finally consume her.

Then some of the police vehicles left. A gurney with someone lying on it covered in a black drape was visible in the dark for a moment as it was wheeled from the house to the back of the black suburban.

Big as it was, its interior was not spacious enough for a person to be propped up on a gurney headed for hospital. It was not an ambulance, and no one was in a hurry. There was no sirens or lights. When it pulled away with all its stealth from the driveway, it seemed to suck the life from the small, quiet bay. CORONER on the plate was visible when its brake lights flashed red before it turned onto the street and away from the small, quiet bay.

We knew then that she had to be gone. Surely, she was now dead. We had become so accustomed to emergency vehicles arriving at all hours, sometimes with lights and sirens; sometimes an ambulance; sometimes a fire engine; sometimes both with the occasional supervisor's vehicle thrown in for good measure. They never stayed long, and she always left the ambulance and walked back into her house.

That early morning, in the dark, we were watching across the street from our front window. Stunned, silently shaking the sleep from our heads, we tried to grasp what we were seeing. Her kids eventually filed out of the house. A few other teens, friends, walked into the small, quiet bay from the greenspace and approached them. Awkward, fumbling hugs were given and received. Masks were not worn.

Two remaining police officers, both wearing masks, spoke with two of her kids before driving away. And then her four kids got back into their vehicles and drove away.

We each had a cup of coffee and cigarettes and tried to decipher what had just unfolded. Then we shuffled back to bed numb, trying to fathom that our neighbour was no longer going to grace our small, quiet bay.

Remembrance Day morning was more solemn than ever before. We watched the scaled back ceremony on national TV. The peals of the piper seemed to squeal louder on the small, quiet bay.

Her youngest daughter, an April child, had always openly chatted with us. She would speak to us often and tell us about her day and ask us about ours. A tiny child not yet in school, she had introduced herself to us when they first moved across the bay a few years ago, but we could never be sure if we heard her name correctly despite asking her to repeat it. She took a shine to my hubby, so he just decided to call her "the boss."

Weeks later, we sadly did find her mother's obituary. Finally, we learned their surname and the names of her children and grandchild. She was a forty-year-old, single, mother of five and new grandmother to baby. The cause of her death was not revealed but it stated that it was sudden. And it finally laid to rest for us the little girl's name.

We felt helpless. We wanted to do something for her kids to let them know that although we did not know each other, we acknowledged their loss.

A few days later one of her boys stopped by the house with his sisters, including the little girl. I had a sympathy card at the ready, addressed to them by name based on the obituary, in case this moment presented itself.

My hubby quickly drove to the grocery store. He bought flowers, a food platter and a small stuffed toy for the little girl. He returned within minutes giving me enough time to place the flowers in a vase, fill it with water and run out the door to deliver to them before they left the small, quiet bay.

The young man, tall and slender, his arms covered in ink, stepped out of the house just as I approached his door. He was caught by surprise. I blurted out that I was his neighbour and that we had read his mother's obituary. I offered our condolences and as I handed him the food platter while I balanced the vase of flowers, I realized in my haste I had forgotten to wear a mask.

DEEP FOCUS

Shayna Stock

close-ups of macaroni noodles

> **long shot of overlapping crises**

i walk with a friend, our bodies
magnetic, our minds
chaperones at a junior high dance
i listen with half of me
with the other half, measure
six feet, spin
impossible equations, divide
risk of spreading virus
by value of my mental health
a futile math with no right answers

> hundreds without homes wander
> the streets, fill the libraries and malls
> seek anywhere to put their bodies
> where they won't be counted, thrown out

i dance with my neighbour through a laptop
we are five blocks apart
face to face in my living room
in her bedroom
longing lengthens the space between us
we are together
full of a kind of intimacy

> addictions offer company,
> release from bodily burdens
> over 1,000 overdoses, 379 deaths
> in one year, and nowhere to go
> to be treated
> like a human

i do an artist residency in my kitchen, end up with
one dozen muffins
a chili in the slow cooker
nine close-ups on my phone of macaroni noodles
and a clean kitchen

moms quit their jobs
if they aren't laid off first
become full-time teachers,
amateur epidemiologists,
crisis management specialists
apply for the benefits, sanitize
the groceries, budget
for half the income, ease
panic attacks, save the crying
for after the kids are asleep

i haul my sewing machine out of storage
sew 31 masks out of an old bed sheet
revel in useful, able hands
recall great-grandma's war garden
her useful hands sinking
squash seeds into soil
three kids at home and probably not glad
to have another thing to keep alive
i don't need kids
someone's got to sew the masks,
bake the muffins, write the poems

soup kitchens double their capacity
but can't let anybody inside
food banks grow broader shoulders, hunch
to hold it all
none of it is enough
nonprofit employees weep
in their cars after work

i hit play on my cbc radio app
call-in show with a microbiologist
isolated voices flock to the phones
like moths to a lighthouse
can the virus spread through my office ventilation system?
should i keep my kids home, visit my mom?
can we hug?
doctor sighs, offers only a dim ray of spiraling maybes

                                        the feds send relief
                                    the province stops theirs
                                     municipality is frantic,
                                   opens a warming shelter
                                  to at least keep people alive
                                     awasiw / they warm up
                                       but they don't sleep
                                       don't get vaccinated
                                        don't get a home

i bake muffins again, eat half a dozen in one day
numbers and time don't matter anyway

                          personal care aides scrub their hands raw,
                                wear out their sneakers and bodies
                                          inmates die, rebel
                          snowbirds get the vaccine in florida
                                       hockey gets $4 million
                                            schools close
                                            bars stay open

i haven't seen mom and dad
for 6 months
8 months
14 months
and counting
not *irl* anyway
grandpa's health is declining

we facetime but
it's not a meal, a hug,
a gentle sharing of space

when does travel count
as essential?

                              neighbours google "mutual aid"
                              learn to administer naloxone
                              bleach the jar before
                  bringing soup to paul in the corner house
                        show interest in their mailboxes again
                              start new group chats, share
                        recipes and mental health support
                  and pics of the view from their windows

i take a too-hot bath
lower my tense body
feel rigid edges relax
let go of the math
sink my ears under
breathe all the way in
watch my soft belly expand
tell myself i'm okay
with the ways my body is changing
wonder if i mean it
sigh loudly
my heartbeat under water
a micro tide
at least
keeping me alive

        *irl – "in real life"

ONE AFTERNOON IN THE WINTER OF OUR DISCONTENT

Helen Mourre

Annabelle looked out her kitchen window at the snow blasted houses on George Street, the result of a ferocious wind two days ago which rampaged throughout the late afternoon, evening, and into the night, leaving little spikes of pain pulsing in her forehead and eyes. No, she reasoned, it's not Covid. The far more likely diagnosis—anxiety. The power had been off all night and the house was just now beginning to warm. It was all too much: the pandemic, the surging case numbers, and then to top it off, a biblical storm.

She'd found the only cure—walking several kilometres a day, no matter the weather. Now her body and her brain and her psyche craved the ritual like an addict. She'd started with one kilometre, worked herself up to two, then three. It was a harmless addiction— low cost, no nasty side effects, respectable.

"I'm going walking, hon," she yelled down to David in the rec room where he was poring over another jigsaw puzzle, *his* addiction of choice. Annabelle thought perhaps he needed therapy, he'd been stuck on this puzzle for weeks now, with a couple dozen pieces left orphaned. It seemed to him that the pieces were all the same and they would kind of fit, but not really, and then he was off on another hunting expedition. Annabelle was no help as she disliked making puzzles and had no talent for it whatsoever.

She set off up the snow-clad street, her studded winter boots grabbing the icy patches, her arms swinging in a pleasant rhythm, legs stretching out, the pain behind her eyes gradually receding. She maneuvered around fallen tree branches and toppled recycling bins all the way up George Street, past Walter Aseltine Elementary where Elliot, her youngest grandson was in grade six. They'd been back in school now for seven days, after closing down for two weeks before Christmas because of a Covid outbreak. She loved hearing the sounds of the children at recess: so bright and innocent and happy, it almost didn't ring true, as if this were a scene from another time, long ago.

At the end of the alley she cut across Jubilee Crescent, and turned onto the Rose Trail, a walking path on the north edge of town with a double row of ash and elm, bordered by a ubiquitous caragana hedge and punctuated with red metal benches. She'd never seen anyone sitting on the benches, but the sight of them made her think that someone might. It was here, on the trail, that the full impact of the storm struck her. The snow had been blown into magnificent dunes, the swooping lines of a master sculptor, while the west side of the trees were covered in long white columns, which seemed to be cut with a knife at even intervals. *Maybe I'm crazy, but I think this is beautiful*, thought Annabelle. She wished she had brought her camera, but then reminded herself to just enjoy the moment for what it was.

It was easier to walk in the alley as the trail was completely blown in and transformed. She slowed, letting unexpected beauty penetrate her soul. Then, at the very edge of her line of vision, she saw them. Four mule deer, spaced two metres apart (they must have gotten the memo) scavenging for whatever had not been plundered by the storm. It was pretty poor pickings. Annabelle wanted to message them: *Don't waste your time.*

As she drew closer, the two smaller deer (they could have been twins) as well as the buck and the doe stopped and stared at her as if *she* was the intruder. Annabelle had never been this close to a wild animal before, had never seen such beautiful eyes, large brown luminescent pools where the mystery of their existence floated. Their absolute stillness was transcendental. The birds that had been gossiping a few moments before quieted. The traffic noise on Marshall Road drifted away. In this pocket of silence Annabelle felt a tingle of alarm, as if she had been told, message coming in, pay attention. They stared at each other, the woman and the deer. And it was Annabelle who had to look away. She turned and continued up the alley, looking back at the deer who now and again glanced her way, but mostly they went back to foraging. They were so patient and willing to stay there and live out the situation to the fullest until something was revealed to them.

The rest of the way home, Annabelle tried to make sense of it. She wanted so badly to believe it meant something. The storm, the transfigured landscape, the pandemic, the deer as they laid claim to her walking trail, the children in the schoolyard; they were all strands from the skein of events in this strange winter. Maybe she would never untangle it, but if she did, it might transform itself into something new and beautiful.

Already at 4:30 in the afternoon, the sun had lost its power and was dropping to the horizon. She could barely see it now, hidden behind the towering new house on the corner of her block.

Her headache gone. Anxiety suppressed. The ache in her soul still there, but lightened somehow. She'd go back home and make a cup of tea for her and David. Perhaps help him find another piece to the puzzle.

MILESTONE

William Robertson

For your birthday
it being your seventieth and all
I've arranged a pair of bluebirds
on a fence. Mountain bluebirds
on a far-off fence.

I know we'd planned a bigger
celebration: a trip to the coast
                walks on the beach
                the still forest's core
but with the pandemic and all,
the fear, the social distancing,
we'll drive out of town, our daughter
behind us in her car, our granddaughters
crowding forward to see—just look
at these Clay-coloured Sparrows
gathered at the road's edge
as Tree Swallows swoop before us.

From an appropriate distance we'll point
to a Yellow-rumped Warbler,
a Meadowlark, eventually a Killdeer.

        And so the day will reveal more birds,
        more breeze, even a wide-spread picnic.

As I say, for your special day
I've arranged these birds.
All we have to do
is find them.

DEADLINE FOR SUBMISSIONS IS MIDNIGHT TODAY

Brenda Schmidt

There's not enough time to properly tell
how little time it took the coyote
to jump the fence this morning or what hell
had torn off the fur from shoulder to throat

well before it got here. It's likely mange,
a run-on sentence of back claws scratching
at mites burrowed for life in the strange
way parasites do. Yes, I'm attaching

everything I've experienced till now
to a suffering predator. So what
next? I ask of the fleeing image. How
can such bareness survive the cold spell? Shut

away in a den? No. This coyote sleeps
with the rest in the open. Its skin weeps.

MAY TO JUNE 2020...A COVID MISCELLANY

Michael Trussler

<u>*Sunday, May 3*</u>

Nurses love the word *perfect*: as in, "do you know what day it is? Per*fect*."

Also, *scoot*: "I'm just going to *scoot* you over there to the other side of the bed" when a patient fouls herself and needs to be bathed. "No worries," the nurse tells her, "I do poop, but not vomit. Francine does vomit." Each nurse pushes the lever on the hand sanitizer on the wall upon leaving the room, and each one remarks that it's still empty.

It seems unaccountably stupid that I'm in the General Hospital while the world is being devastated by Covid.

Tequila + chronic depression and generalized anxiety + new and unfamiliar meds ⟶ my own private ecological catastrophe. I'm having what used to be called *a nervous breakdown* and now I need to be kept under observation for several days.

Don't get me wrong, this collapse was a long time coming.

<u>*Monday, May 4*</u>

An announcement on the intercom wakes me up: *Code Blue on the Heliport.* Chairs scrape out in the hall. People rush. When they hear these words, do staff first picture the colour or does the message's urgency overrule the way each person summons an image of blue?

The man in the other bed is 84. He had suddenly turned blind when he was 21. Upon the delivery of food this morning, he kept calling out "I can't find my breakfast" because the nurse's aide had put it in a different place than before.

David Foster Wallace's *Infinite Jest* is the perfect book for reading while I'm here. The first time I read it, a few years ago, I was also in a deplorable state. I put the book down for my daily ECG.

I'm told that there don't seem to be any long-term medical consequences, and I want to go home, but I'm told I'm going to be transferred to the Mental Health unit. What if, as an adult, I refuse to go? I ask. "Then we have to have you committed."

Tuesday, May 5

A string of dental floss, the nurse in the psych ward handing it to me, my own supply confiscated in case I tried to use it to perform self-harm.

A woman walks by whose bare feet look like they've been hacked out of an El Greco painting.

Only weeks ago, enraged Brazilians stood on their balconies and beat large spoons against pots and pans to protest their president's inept and callous response to the Covid virus.

Wednesday, May 6

Each morning upon waking, you're given a blood test, and then three times throughout the day your blood pressure is taken. Meds come in a small paper cup to be taken with water in a Dixie cup. Just like in the movies, the nurse looks directly at you until you've swallowed the pills.

I'm reminded of the twentieth century because when someone walks by speaking aloud it's because he's mentally ill, not because he's wearing a Bluetooth.

Someone in what's called *Group* (a circle of people sitting across from each other in a small room) is bi-polar and what he most wants to do is rub ropes of wool in his hands, pet them because his fingers were *feeling very sensitive* and the wool was soft and soothing to the touch. Another person bursting suddenly into tears as he recalls fishing with his father and brother and when the session is over he asks the leader for a hug – but of course Covid denies that.

Thursday, May 7

I'm discharged. Following the nurse to the locked door, I realize I've not been outside for nearly an entire week. A messy man approaches from the parking lot as I wait for my wife to pick me up. He wants me to buy some art he's made—stick people shaded in various colours and two fire engines—but I tell him truthfully I have no money. "How long have you been in there?" he asks, nodding at the exit from the Mental Health Wing. "That's a hard place to get out of," he says, moving away as a security guard approaches to warn him off hospital property. What memories is he drawing upon?

Saturday, May 9

I finish Albert Camus's *The Plague*. Originally published in 1947, the novel was meant to allegorize the Nazi occupation, though it's startlingly prescient of Covid. "What's natural is the microbe," Camus writes, of the plague-ridden city of Oran.

One character refers to a criminal he'd seen in court many years earlier and says that he *looked like a yellow owl scared blind by too much light*. A few pages earlier, the reader will have come across these words: *In fact, it comes to this: nobody is capable of thinking about anyone.*

Tuesday, May 12

When Britain's lockdown began, a woman with Alzheimer's (who has responded to her condition by discussing the disease at symposia and hospitals all over England for the past few years) blogs her fear that her dementia will worsen because she's no longer able to experience the mental stimulation travel provides.

Thursday, May 14

My ten-year-old son, Jakob, and I have been going for walks most mornings around Wascana Lake, our binoculars hanging around our necks for birdwatching along the lake. The ones he's got were originally mine; I bought them when I was fourteen with money I earned shoveling snow and cutting grass. The Snowbird jets pass overhead, flying east and then west over Regina, their purpose ostensibly is to lift people's spirits because of Covid. Heading for the trees, we stay off the path, which has signs indicating that people have to walk around the lake clockwise to maintain social distancing.

Some twenty minutes later, we hear, and then see, the first male Baltimore oriole of the season, the bright orange of his plumage the colour of an incandescent plastic pumpkin, the sort kids carry on Halloween for their candy. Jakob has never seen this bird species before. He wonders if we'll still be in lockdown when Halloween comes. And then he says that Halloween this year will special: there will be a full moon on the thirty-first.

Time has always obsessed me, especially when I think of all that has happened on certain special days. But now, this concern about time is more simple: it's panic about the future. I can't help myself from asking Google when the next full moon will occur on Halloween. 2039. If I make it, I'll be almost eighty and Jakob will be at the end of his twenties. Given that 2020 is looking to be the hottest year on record, what will his world be like in terms of global warming? Will there be another pandemic in between now and then? One that is more lethal?

Today is my father's eighty-first birthday.

Sunday, May 17

One of the Snowbirds crashes in Kamloops, killing two people. Standing nearby the dirty kitchen sink, my wife Amy and I discuss whether we should let Jakob know about this accident: being unable to go to school or play with his friends has weighed down his spirits.

Monday, May 18

Covid is gaining momentum in the U.S. (over 70,000 deaths) but cases are low in South Korea (under 300). South Korea paid attention to SARS. David Thompson observes: *The truth is that the Korean government and its citizens did something simple, admirable, and all too rare: they suffered from history, and they learned from it.*

Suffered from history: in 1980, May 18 was a Sunday and in South Korea troops fired on students, marking the Gwangju Massacre, and across the ocean at the very same time Mt. St. Helens blew the day apart, lava and ash covering Harry Truman (not the U.S. president) and his 16 cats. Harry was a former World War I pilot who refused to budge from the place he made his own on Spirit Lake. And many dead students were lying in a perfectly straight line because that's how they fell.

Because history sometimes wears riding spurs to bed and at the same time its swirling ash pounds bullet holes into the ecology of a day's deranged and vanishing architecture.

Tuesday, May 19

Turkey vultures make sweeping circles overhead for the second evening in a row. Apart from American pelicans and the rare eagle, no other bird soars with such majesty over southern Saskatchewan. Something invisible in the messy sky has opened and let them through.

Police forces begin to observe an upsurge of the online sexual abuse of children owing to Covid increasing the amount of time they spend on computer screens.

<u>*Wednesday, May 20*</u>
An electronic billboard on Albert Street announces: *If there was no change, there wouldn't be any butterflies.*

Ummn, OK. Really?

And from Walpola Rahula's *What the Buddha Taught*:

"The conception of *dukkha* may be viewed from three aspects: (1) *dukkha* as ordinary suffering (*dukkha-dukkha*), (2) *dukkha* as produced by change (*viparināma-dukkha*) and *dukkha* as conditioned states (*samkhāra-dukkha*)."

Which means we don't own anything, especially our health, but it doesn't mean we shouldn't be attentive to daily instances of the flamboyant.

My niece, a nurse who has been *deployed* in a care home, has tested positive for Covid. She needs to self-quarantine in her apartment for two weeks.

<u>*Thursday, May 21*</u>
Today two items came in the mail: a bill for the ambulance that came on May 1 and Gareth Hinds's ingenious graphic novel of Edgar Allan Poe's writing.

The first story is "The Masque of the Red Death."

Because he's been kept from school, Jakob and I have been reading much of Hinds's work. Strange that Poe doesn't dwell on the strangest of experiences: the passing of time. Recent studies in addiction suggest that people like Poe are entombed in the present, being incapable of mediating the present with an ongoing "life narrative" that conjoins the past, present and future.

$325 for the ambulance, but what of those who couldn't afford this bill, or those for whom no ambulance comes at all?

When I played Jakob "The Raven" from the Alan Parsons Project debut album *Tales of Mystery and Imagination* (1976), he said it was all right, but not [his] favourite. He far prefers the drawing Hinds had made of the bird with figures of skulls and bony claws almost hidden in its plumage.

<u>*Monday, May 25*</u>
Jakob has become very blue because of Covid isolation and my stay in the hospital.

Desperate to shift his mood, Amy has taken him to get some donuts and then to the railway bridge where he can shoot cherry pits into the creek below with his new slingshot. Two trains, the first coming out of the blur and going west, the other east, take them utterly by surprise. And then shortly afterwards, a cop in a ghost car shows up, wanting to know if they'd seen kids playing on the tracks. No, she said, telling me later she's never lied to a police officer before.

It's difficult to fathom but I spoke with someone on the street who believes that Trump is right and Covid is most likely a hoax.

Gilles Deleuze advises that we should "become worthy of what happens to us." How is one supposed to do this exactly?

Wednesday, May 27
The Sunday *New York Times* arrives. The entire first page (then 12-14) lists the nearly 100,000 names of Americans who have died of Covid plus a brief description of their lives: Dante Dennis Flagello, *62, Rome, Ga., his greatest accomplishment was his relationship with his wife.*

Change.org has just sent an email asking subscribers to sign a petition protesting an online company that sells baby turtles encased in resin to be used as paperweights. Online shoppers have an interest in paperweights?

Thursday, May 28
I don't feel entirely here. It's as though when I look at what's in front of me there's a narrow, vertical band of something missing off to the right. Picture a long, straight line of light, but the line isn't made of light so much as it's a shaft of non-colour, non-presence, as though something on the other side of what's visible has sucked away the space holding whatever this line is.

Friday, May 27
Family movie night. It's Amy's turn. We watch Wes Anderson's *Isle of Dogs* for the second time, the first was when it played at the public library when it came out.

Sunday, May 31
No systemic racism in the U.S., claims a Trump advisor. People protesting George Floyd's murder and wearing masks for Covid, not only in American cities but now in Canada and England too.

In everyday experience, months somehow evaporate into each other.

In normal life, few people seem to be dismayed by this. These days though, everyone is inside their own brain fog, and we complain about the way time stumbles and sleep walks us past every new day.

Monday June 1 thru Wednesday June 3
Saskatchewan eases its lockdown, and has opened up its provincial parks to its own citizens: we go camping at Duck Mountain Provincial Park. Showers are closed. Campfires are forbidden, so Amy buys an old-fashioned charcoal barbecue with a round lid. Jakob cooks us hot dogs.

Despite ticks, the birding has been wonderful. Eagles, Over 40 Red-necked grebes. Loons. A lone Franklin's gull. A common merganser. Best: the killdeer with three chicks. The loons glisten with water droplets. The black their heads retain after diving isn't an ordinary black: it's a preternatural dye that shimmers with refulgent austerity.

Will animal life recuperate because of a lack of human activity in the world?

Seventy km-per-hour winds arrive the night of the third and so we decide to return home, one day early. South of Melville, as we drive through complete darkness, Amy shouts: "A moose! Stop!" Impossible to stop, so I swerve, just avoiding its back legs. It's a male, his body at least a metre higher than our bug-smeared, white car.

A brindled mass flashing in the headlights.

The human realm is like the tip of a hair on the body of a horse—Zhuangzi

If somewhere along the drive I'd gone two seconds faster, we'd be hospitalized or worse. If the moose had delayed his saunter across the road by two or three seconds, the same. I'm shaking as I drive, but I know that my mind will get lazy when it tries to acknowledge this near-event-of-dying of the three of us. As each day turns into another one, my thoughts will inevitably leave that moment stranded back there on the highway.

Friday, June 5
Laurie Anderson's seventy-third birthday. And thirty-one years ago in Beijing, the Tiananman Square protests come to a bloody climax.

My sister and the man who would become her husband, then a med student, were in Beijing that spring, and saw the Statue of Democracy. She sent a postcard of a scroll painting featuring some bamboo that's in front of me as I type.

A single man facing four tanks...where is Tank Man and is he well? Well and where? And how is it that time is scrubbed clean of what happens? And one day Covid will be a memory that's on nobody's playlist, cultural memory is a latent ratio measuring active oblivion: chance.

What is it like to be in Wuhan and remember this day?

My sister's husband is now part of a team of doctors in charge of how Calgary's Foothills Hospital is managing Covid.

Apart from catching Covid, what concerns me the most is something Camus says about the citizens of Oran once the plague had passed. Denial replaced their earlier fear: "Calmly they denied, in the teeth of evidence, that *we* had ever known a crazy world in which men were killed off like flies."

When a vaccine arrives and life returns to normal, will we carry on as we did before or will we recognize the societal failures Covid has revealed? This may be my mood disorders speaking, but I don't know if we have the courage to face how flimsy our grasp of what's headed our way actually is.

Notes:

Italics are my own.
- Quotations from Albert Camus's *The Plague* are from the Stuart Gilbert translation.
- David Thompson "What's Behind South Korea's Covid-19 Exceptionalism?" www.theatlantic.com/ideas/archive/2020/05/whats-south-koreas-secret/611215/
- The information regarding the Gwangju Massacre is from *Human Acts* by Han Kang. A description of Harry Truman is easily found online.
- The citation from Zhuangzi is from David E. Cooper, *Convergence with Nature: A Daoist Perspective*. Green Books, 2012.

WITNESS

Denise Wilkinson

We hide in ostrich fern, wait for the strangers to pass. We have come for the blessing of aloneness, the marvel of holding the moment, of communing with Balsam fir and Jack pine. It is our first hike on the Narrows Peninsula trail, the first summer of our kids not at home, the first year of staying close in a world pandemic.

Ahead, an impossibly large dragonfly rests, body spotted pastel blue, eyes teal, face new-grass-green. He lets me take photos, then lumbers into flight, heavy from the mosquito feast of July. We stumble on, forest opening to shallow beach and mild waves. Distant rumble and brooding clouds warn, yet we stay. How can we fear in this sanctuary, our breath christened by earth and water and air?

Breathing is becoming. Breathing, being breathed, uniting . . .

But there is supper to make, so we turn to faded boardwalk and branches and moss, pass unearthed roots and lichen berries, back toward pavement and people. As we go, we take, and keep, this sacred space inside.

TWO RAINBOWS

Joan Crate

Sun and rain today, a mediation of weather in two rainbows,
one solid as dream, the other thin as my clawed skin.

For the third day in a row, a golden eagle soars overhead
one glinting eye on her nestlings, the other scouring rock
for young marmots. She swoops, a lethal
miracle flapping from the tips of my fingers
through veins, wings in my eyes, ears, feathers
stroking the face of sun, the ghost of you
clutching every cell.

Honour song of sky, gospel choir of flight and wind,
bring me this, only this: everything
I can't hold.

When sleep won't come
I crunch Smarties between loose fillings and ask *Alexa*
to play the blues as she listens in on my whispers to the dead
of night while sticking Band-Aids over mosquito bites, scrapes and rips,
lesions in my brain where you have been pulled out of me. Nothing

is more than I can bear.

COFFEE IN A TIME OF QUARANTINE

Aliza Prodaniuk

On day twenty-three of lockdown, I needed a latte.

I needed a latte like air. Like plants need sun. Like my headache required caffeine. But I only had tea.

I poured boiling water into a mug and plunged the tea bag up and down. I was angrier than when I was laid off because my client's businesses closed due to Covid-19 restrictions. My career as a "content writer" was precarious at best. Now I was a temp writing blogs for Mattressville, and I thought nothing could make me angrier than that. Leafy particles spun around the mug, taunting me as if to say, "drink, bitch."

I closed my eyes and imagined rich-bodied espresso poured over stiff peaks of frothed milk. I took a sip of hot salad water and almost—almost —tasted the bitter-sweet liquid I longed for. A rehydrated leaf launched into my throat and latched onto my uvula. I coughed, tears dripping down my cheeks. I dumped the tea into the sink, dropping the mug in after it, and heard the satisfying crack of ceramic on metal. Enough was enough; today, I'd have a latte.

I crossed the street from my condo to my favourite coffee shop, Grupettos. It was a 'hole in the wall' joint only accessible from the alley beside the health-food grocery store where it operated out of a converted stockroom. Grupettos didn't have a sign to mark its location. Karl, the proprietor, didn't need one. He served the best joe in town, and the gang of middle-aged cyclists and artists that frequented the place knew it, too.

However, Grupettos was closed.

Next, I tried Delirious Coffee Roasters, but it was closed, too.

I tried the Starbucks across the street, to the same effect.

I tried the Muddy Cup, The Espresso Cafe, Java the Hut, Deja Brew, but there wasn't a latte to be had.

I walked down King St. towards home. Me without coffee was like the closed boutiques with unsold spring stock, galleries with unviewed paintings, and restaurants without food. I passed two cops checking doors and shining flashlights through windows. It was like cops without petty crime!

"Watch it!"

I jumped, narrowly avoiding a collision with a woman coming out of the Grupettos alleyway.

"I'm sorry," I said, but she was already rounding the corner.

I stopped. Could it be? It was just a flash. I'd seen it for no more than a second. The ninety-degree hook of the woman's arm held in perfect balance, bouncing to the weight of sixteen ounces. An airy lightness I knew well, concealed behind a scarf draped too precisely over the front of her jacket. And then a slight flutter of the wind. That's when I saw it. Hidden behind her scarf was a white to-go cup—the kind used at Grupettos.

Karl had not forsaken me after all.

I stepped one foot into the alley when I made eye contact with the cops. I smiled. They smiled. They took a step forward. I took a step back.

"Beautiful day out," one said.

"Words can't espresso how I feel."

The cops looked at each other. "Well, stay safe."

"Thanks a latte! I mean, *a lot*."

Once inside my condo, I grabbed my binoculars and went out to my balcony, which offered a perfect view of the Grupettos alleyway. I'd have a latte, even if it killed me!

*

That night, I returned to the alley to look for clues. I found a piece of paper taped to Grupettos' door, filled with cryptic coffee correspondences that gave me insight into how Karl's clientele was giving and receiving orders.

Theo, the usual?

Renetta, was that baby juice or soy?

Dave, I got your message about the tall blonde. Tell me more.

Unsure if Karl knew me by name, I jotted my order on a sticky note, signed it, and slid the paper under the door. The next night, when a new list appeared, I wasn't on it.

I couldn't eat, sleep, or write. Meanwhile, I was inundated with emails and calls from my freelance agent as more Mattressville deadlines slipped by.

I was an inmate on my fifth-floor balcony. During the day, I watched people emerge from the alley, their cups concealed in bags, by scarves, and in the case of one woman, her child's hood. The night was my furlough when I would return to the alley to take note of the latest sign.

Mia, did you get your belly warmer?

Ten for the pair of drawers, Rahul.

All out of your usual sinkers and suds, Kwasi.

And then, on day forty-one of lockdown, Karl made a mistake I'd waited for. He left a time: *Ringo, gotta change your pickup to two tomorrow.*

You better believe I was waiting when Ringo arrived. A tall, hooded figure turned into the alley. I crossed the street from my condo and watched Grupettos' door crack open long enough for a white cup to slide out. When Ringo bent to grab it, I approached. He took one look at me and started running. I chased him to the end of the alley, where he jumped the fence into the parking lot on the other side like a spring-loaded giraffe, and then he raised his cup, a metaphoric F-U.

I felt defeated. Crushed! Finished! My one chance, *gone.* I banged my fists against the door, and, to my surprise, it opened. Inside, the lights were off, and the tables were pushed to one side. The room was illuminated by a sliver of light escaping through the sliding security door that separated Grupettos from the health-food grocery store. In the dim light, I could see Karl with his back to me, standing in front of the copper-plated espresso machine, red-plaid shirt pushed to his elbows.

I could have cried from the nearest rooftop!

"This is heaven!" I said, inhaling every note of the coffee flavour wheel in one heavenly breath.

"I'm flattered, but we're closed for the end of the world."

"I need a latte."

"You're gonna have to get your fix somewhere else."

"Everywhere else is closed."

"So am I."

"What about Ringo?"

Karl poured espresso into a cup and clicked the lid into place. He didn't turn as he flipped a white cup in the air, caught it, and started on the next order. "Ringo's on the list."

"Put me on the list."

"How do I know you're not a rat?"

"I've never been a rat."

"Only a slave to the bean won't rat."

"Oh, I'm a slave."

"But are you a regular? Only regulars are allowed on the list."

"I haven't been regular since quarantine started."

"Well, coffee won't help you."

"I need a latte!"

"Look, I'm not your saviour. The cops have been checking businesses, and the grocer is breathing down my neck. I'm barely staying afloat as is, and the grocer is still expecting rent and half the utilities even though I haven't flushed the toilet, answered the phone, or turned on a light in weeks." Karl clicked a lid on the second cup and turned towards me. He wiped condensation from his thick, black-framed glasses with a thumb. "Whole Milk Latte! Why didn't you say it was you?"

I opened my mouth to respond, but my knees buckled, and I fell into the counter. I felt weak having those full cups of coffee so close, yet so far, like when you need to pee and you can't get your pants down fast enough.

"Whoa there, Whole Milk Latte!" Karl said and pushed a cup towards me. "No need for dramatics."

I lifted the cup to my lips and took a shaky sip. I couldn't stop. Within seconds, I chugged the entire cup. I used my fingers to scoop out the foam, and then I grabbed the second coffee. When I'd polished the second cup, Karl gave me a nod.

"Ten even, and I'll put you on the list."

I returned the next day, and then the day after that until I was spending almost forty bucks per week on contraband coffee.

*

On day sixty-three of lockdown, Grupettos closed.

It was early, and I'd just picked up my order. I was just about to exit the alley when I heard voices. I took a peek around the corner and saw a cop coming down the sidewalk, trailed by the health-food grocery store owner, Karen, dressed in full PPE. I took a step back.

"I'm telling you, he's selling coffee right under your nose!" said Karen.

"Alright, calm down," the cop replied. As they passed, I recognized him as the freckled guy who usually got his coffee order after me on Thursdays.

"I won't be calm!"

"Alright, alright!"

"Not alright! My neighbour's fourteen-year-old daughter came home with coffee yesterday. How do I explain that to a mother?"

"Your neighbour's kid could be doing worse."

"Really? That's what you have to say?" Karen huffed. "And during a pandemic!"

"I can talk with Karl, but at the end of the day, you choose whether he stays or goes."

When I thought they were well past the alley, I made for the exit, but I collided with Karen, crushing my coffee cup into my shirt. The nutty smell of espresso filled the air. I stumbled back against the brick wall. Karen lifted her face shield, and sniffed a wet spot on her jacket, her eyes going light and then dark, light then dark.

"Coffee!" she said.

I looked at the freckle-faced cop, and he looked at the sky.

"Where did you get that?"

"H-home."

"You're using a to-go cup?"

I was speechless. Karen turned towards the cop. "She's using a to-go cup. Where did she get a to-go cup?"

That night, no note appeared on Grupettos' door, and the next day, Karl and his espresso machine were gone.

*

On day eighty of quarantine, I needed a latte.

I'd overdone it with my latte intake, sure. I knew it. My bank account knew it. The yellowish colour of my teeth knew it. Not to mention the constant headache I'd experienced since Grupettos closed. My cravings showed throughout my life.

Once I'd caught a glimpse of myself in the mirror and was shocked. I had dark circles under my eyes like someone had painted my binoculars' eye holes with black ink. My hair looked like a greasy ball of spaghetti.

The calls and emails from my agent also stopped, and that was just as well. I'd already decided that I'd never touch a single article about Tempur-pedic, Purple, adjustable beds, or any other spring-loaded, memory foam mattress offering sleep nirvana again.

I raised my binoculars to my face, expecting to scan an empty street, but something was different. A brightly coloured mass stirred on the hazy summer horizon. It came closer, stopped at the intersection, weaved through traffic. They weren't just cyclists; they were a swarm of men in 'make your grandma blush' spandex suits. It could only mean one thing.

With all the ding-dong, ring-a-ling bike bells, it didn't take me long to find Karl. In the next plaza, between a tchotchke shop and the police station, the newly minted travelling contraband coffee cart was jammed into the cheese store's doorway.

Laughter and coffee flowed like a soda stream.

"Whole Milk Latte!" Karl said when it was my turn to order. He looked me up and down. "You missed me a lot, eh?"

I rolled my eyes. "How'd you swing the cheese store?"

"Old friends of mine. They sell me my milk."

"What about the police?"

Karl pointed, and I saw freckle-face laughing with a few bikers. "Everyone has their drug."

For a few weeks, things were good. I spent my days in the plaza, writing. I wrote about the contraband coffee cart and its customers, and I felt inspired for the first time by my work.

But Karen just couldn't mind her own business, and one morning I found her fighting with Karl in the plaza.

"You just don't know when to quit, do you?" Karen said, shaking her head.

"What do you care? I'm not your renter anymore."

"No, but you are breaking the law, and, as a responsible citizen, I will not stand idly by and watch you put people at risk!"

"I get the sense that you're a tea person. That's your problem," Karl replied.

"And that means?"

"Coffee people are less high strung and aggressive."

"High strung and aggressive!?"

"You're very high strung and aggressive. I can whip you up something special, you'll see."

"No, you'll see, Karl. You'll see!"

The next day she came back with the freckle-faced cop, who did nothing. The day after that, she came with city officials.

I was there when the OPP finally came to stick Karl with a big, hefty Covid fine. But the travelling contraband coffee cart was already gone, leaving a bright pink poster in its place.

Karen, the cops, city officials, the bikers, and I all crowded around the crudely drawn map of King St. with all its side-streets and alleys. A blue line ran along the streets like a river starting at the cheese store, and ended in a large X behind what looked to be the bank.

We all took off at once. Karen in her Dodge Caravan, The OPP in cruisers, city officials in cars, bikers on bikes and me on foot. I zipped down sidewalks, side-stepped through outdoor patios, and cut through parking lots, reaching the bank before anyone else.

There was Karl in a bright red 1950s-style food truck.

"You only have about a minute!"

"Chill out, Whole Milk Latte." He started on what would've been my latte.

"They're coming!"

"Who's coming?"

"Everyone!"

"Everyone?"

"I mean, everyone!"

Sirens filled the air. Karl slammed the order window shut. He jumped into the driver's seat as Karen sped into the parking lot. He cranked the van into drive, flew over the curb, and was gone.

Even after the OPP and city officials gave up, the chase continued. Karen went one way, Karl went the other. Bikers went one way, I went the other. You never knew where you'd find the travelling contraband coffee van, and there didn't seem to be a place that Karl could be where Karen couldn't follow.

*

On day 110 of lockdown, the trail went cold. I wandered the streets searching for the travelling contraband coffee van when a biker pedalled by.

"Hey!" I yelled.

"I don't give lifts," the biker said, wheeling around.

"I don't want a lift; I want a latte."

He raised his eyebrows. "I might be able to help."

"Will you?"

"Are you a rat?"

"I've never been a rat."

"You don't look like a rat."

"That's because I'm not a rat."

Karen's Dodge Caravan turned onto King St. and slowly drove past. The biker studied a window display and I looked at my phone.

"I need a latte," I said through gritted teeth.

"Try the alley behind the library," the biker mumbled back.

By the time I got to the library, there was just another map waiting for me that led to more dead-ends.

Finally, on day 115 of lockdown, I found Karl parked between the outdoor equipment store and Dave's Fine Footwear having a heated argument with Karen.

"If you don't stop selling coffee, I'm going to kill you!" Karen said.

I leaned against the coffee truck. "Get the lady a latte, on me."

"I drink tea!" she responded.

"Sadist," I said.

"Vegan," Karl said.

"I'm calling the police," Karen said.

"They've already been here today," Karl said, smiling.

Karen got into her van and slammed the door. The engine roared to life. Then she did something unexpected. She drove pedal-to-the-medal towards Karl's van. And I, desperate to save my only caffeine source, lunged between them.

*

On day 365 of lockdown, I left the hospital where I'd finished writing my first creative writing piece and decided it would be my full-time gig.

Karl found a permanent location, rebranding as Domestique. Karen was incarcerated for her hit and run, and Covid restrictions were being slowly lifted.

The day I returned home, I needed a latte. When I walked into Domestique, Karl smiled from behind his espresso machine.

"What's your damage?" Karl said.

"Whole milk latte," I responded.

Karl flipped a cup in the air and caught it.

It was a perfect day for coffee in a time of quarantine.

IS IT WRONG

Anne Lazurko

To wish my mother dead
months ago when pneumonic
phlegm wheezed in
ancient lungs too weak to
persuade a capable
cough that might end her
suffocation, our mingled tears,
hands twined with hers
infantile, pulsing fingertips a reminder
time moves always toward
the last breath, hers
only the final note
of the meadowlark's song,
heart-bursting as life.

Directive signed –
no heroic measures –
clinical calculation made
at a more lucid age when
she imagined choice was real,
instead a teaspoon of simple
fermented mold to see if
miraculously it works, brings
her shuffling back no less
mortal or bedridden,
no more able to feed herself,
but anew the vigour
in those cloud blue eyes
trilling, triumphant.

But now…
this corona renders her

loyal subject to a silent
Emperor imprisoning her,
banished to crouch in fearful wait
of crow's dark shadow, lonely
lids shut tight, willing
infection to pass over the lintel
painted lamb's blood
red with prayers and hope
it cannot enter this room,
this care home where care-givers
care like never before
to isolate and protect her
vapour thin skin
covered bones –
from me.

And should solitude fail her,
ask her to bear the crown
amidst hovering hazmat ghosts,
latex hands caressing soft
the slack contours of her face, a
momentary sorrow at this passing
before the next, heroes needed
elsewhere; they will not
witness her rheumatic talons
reaching to grasp the aura,
place the ring to wreathe
her eagle's head with crest
of fractured light and look,
there she soars proudly
solo into that good night,
touching the divine, regal, dignified
because my monarch always
knew her worth.

A GIFT FOR THESE DIFFICULT DAYS

Lynda Monahan

I would give you silence
,wrapped in soft cloth
quiet as flannel
you could touch to your cheek
hold it close
when the world's suffering
is too much with you

you could unfold that silence
and find inside
the forest's deep hush
be there among the tall cool trees
in the deepening shadows
the delicate movements of deer

I would give you solitude
an aloneness which is not lonely
but a gift of rest

for you I would make the world move quietly
give you the slow gold of a sunset
lingering over the lake
the lisp of water at the shore

these gentle rhythms
I would give you
the soft brush of a breath
in the deep stillness of snow

GAMBLE

Jenny Ryan

While you're frozen in this panic, in this
        present tense
your little boy is in the basement
stringing up lights
pushing seeds into potting soil
reaching for the watering can
and placing a bet on spring

ON THE EVE OF HALLOWE'EN

P. J. *Worrell*

Elizabeth I

On a homestead at Rhein, Saskatchewan, Elizabeth and her husband, Heinrich, grew grain and vegetables, and raised cattle, pigs, and chickens to feed their six children. They drew water from a well, cooked on a wood stove, heated with furnace oil, washed clothes on a washboard, used an outhouse, and owned a team of horses to pull a plow, buggy, and sleigh. Their day-to-day lives were much the same as those of other German immigrants who had arrived on the prairies from Russia early in the twentieth century and were spared the Bolshevik massacre.

Although women had earned the right to vote in 1916, neither Elizabeth nor Heinrich voted in the 1917 election because they could not read or write English. By then, the population of Saskatchewan had grown to 700,000 due to immigration from Germany, the United States, and the Scandinavian countries.

News of *Influenza* reached Rhein in 1918, causing them to worry about their youngest daughter Lillian's barking cough. They took her by horse and buggy the 36 miles to Yorkton to see a doctor. He prescribed medicine for croup, and explained how to make a croupette. Before leaving Yorkton, Heinrich bought the October 1 edition of the *Regina Leader*. He could make sense of the word "flu" in the headline.

Heinrich constructed a dome-shaped frame over Lillian's bed and covered it with canvas. Elizabeth set a pot of boiling water on the floor for the steam to rise into an opening in the tent.

Heinrich took the newspaper to the Justice of Peace in Rhein. He read aloud: "Dr. Seymour, Provincial Health Commissioner, will search a train bound from eastern Canada for signs of the Spanish Influenza amongst the passengers. Some passengers with symptoms had already been removed from the train in Winnipeg. Preventative measures to stop the spread of the disease include isolation and the wearing of masks."

Lillian's cough improved and she no longer gasped for breath, but the medicine ran out and she was still unwell. The doctor in Yorkton gave them a different concoction on their second visit, and advised them to keep brandy on hand in case either of them caught the Spanish Flu. Heinrich picked up the October 15 edition of the *Regina Leader.*

Back in Rhein, the JP read: "Dr. Seymour is asking any nurses or physicians available to help with the epidemic to report to his office.... To avoid getting the flu he suggests to avoid crowds, not to sneeze or cough close to another person and not to use sprays or gargles unless suggested by a physician. The hospitals, including the isolation hospital are all full with cases of the Spanish Flu. Many medical professionals are ill.... The situation at the R.N.W.M.P. barracks has improved, with only one death and no other severe cases in the last three days."

Lillian recovered fully, but Heinrich and two of their other children became ill. A midwife came to the house wearing a mask and confirmed their fear that it was the Spanish Flu. She told about children who had died and the neighbour who had fallen dead on his way from the barn to the house. "There are no funerals," she said, "only burials." Hospitals in Yorkton and Regina were full, and a home had opened in Moose Jaw for children whose parents were too ill to care for them. She warned them to stay out of other people's houses because the disease was extremely contagious.

Heinrich was confined to bed, coughing day and night. Elizabeth steamed him with eucalyptus oil in boiling water, applied putrid mustard plasters to his chest, and spooned Bishop's Blackberry Brandy between his dry, cracked lips.

Ten-year-old Henry took over feeding and watering the farm animals. With instructions from his father, he put up the croupette over his sick brother and sister's bed.

They had no way of knowing about the shortage of wooden coffins, or that churches, cafés, and pool halls in Regina had been closed, or that gatherings of more than twenty-five people were prohibited, with the threat of $50 fines.

In answer to Elizabeth's prayers (so she believed), her husband and children survived, but Heinrich remained frail. His lungs had been weakened, he tired easily, and he was unable to do any physical labour.

He rented out their land to a man named George the following spring, and made plans for a house to be built in the village of Rhein. His intention was to give up farming, move his family to the village, and live off income from the rent and livestock.

At the end of July 1919, Heinrich went in to check on the progress of the house. He took Lillian along. He came home with an inexpensive necklace for Elizabeth's birthday, treats for each of the children, and a newspaper.

When he kissed Elizabeth and gave her the present, she said, "*Dumm Esel*," scolding him for wasting money.

Young Henry read the July 23 *Regina Morning Leader* to his parents, mistaking some words and skipping over others. He began with news about the Spanish Flu, then weather, then an article about a by-election in nearby Pelly. "Sarah Ramsland is making a strong run in Pelly canvassing for votes to succeed her husband, Magnus, who died last year of Influenza. Accompanied by a woman friend, the two drove their own car. It's a rough country, with many bad roads, and the making of the trip successfully has proved to people that a woman can get around and represent them even under difficulties.... Liberal Premier William Melville Martin was quoted, saying this would give the widow an income for her and the children."

Elizabeth, busily hand-stitching a scrap quilt while listening, shook her head, incredulous. "*Was nekst?*"

They later learned that Sarah Ramsland had indeed been elected as the first woman ever in the Legislative Assembly of Saskatchewan.

Heinrich's cough worsened and at times he couldn't catch his breath. By October, he was again bed-ridden. Elizabeth sat by his bed at night, praying, "*Gott im himmel, bitte....*"

He whispered, "*Wenn ich sterbe, gehe in....*" He was instructing her to move into the new house when it was ready, if he didn't make it.

She shushed him in a rough tone of voice, "*Halt den Mund*," and continued praying.

On October 31, young Henry was carrying a pail of milk from the barn to the house in the dark after milking cows. He stopped to watch a bat flying around the roof of the house again and again. He didn't know of the superstition that a bat circling a house is a sign of an impending death.

On the eve of Hallowe'en in 1919, while pranksters knocked over outhouses in Rhein, Heinrich died at the age of thirty-four.

Elizabeth fell forward. At first she was silent. Numb. Then she wailed, but not so loud as to wake the children. She wanted to be alone with her husband, to be intimate with him while his body was still warm. The patchwork quilt stifled her high-pitched keening and absorbed her tears.

Eventually, her death wail collapsed into a moan and she fell asleep face first on the mattress.

The H1N1 virus, called the Spanish Flu, killed 5,000 people in Saskatchewan, 55,000 in Canada, many young and hardy like Heinrich. The major cause of death was not the flu itself, but rather pneumonia in patients like him who had been weakened by the flu.

Elizabeth was a thirty-year-old widow with six children ages two to eleven. Why had God not answered her prayers?

Henry had to quit school in Grade Six to care for the livestock and help his mother around the farm. At the end of the work day, he would read Zane Grey—*The Last of the Plainsmen* or *The Rustlers of Pecos County* —by the light of a coal oil lamp. That winter, temperatures dipped to 45 degrees below zero on the Fahrenheit thermometer.

Elizabeth did move the family into Rhein in spring. Lillian showed her a footprint in the concrete at the base of the front step. Heinrich had removed one of her shoes and socks and pressed her little foot into the wet cement that summer day she had accompanied him to town.

Elizabeth took in boarders, a school teacher and the Lutheran minister, to supplement the rental income from the farm. Henry travelled the three miles out to the farm daily to fill the troughs for the cattle, pigs, and chickens, and to milk the cows. He was also responsible for the horses kept in a corral behind the new house. Elizabeth's children would later say, "Mother ruled the roost with an iron fist." After the younger ones were in bed, her eldest daughter, Sarah, taught her to read and write English.

George, the man who rented the farm land, was left with three children when his wife died. He was ready to quit farming after drought, a grasshopper infestation, crop failure, and widowhood. He asked Elizabeth to marry him and move to Winnipeg, where he had secured a job. She agreed.

Leaving behind Lillian's footprint tugged at Elizabeth's heart when she sold the house in Rhein in 1925. Her four youngest children went along to Winnipeg. Henry and Sarah, almost adults by then, took over the farm.

George and Elizabeth's blended family arrangement did not survive. The Great Depression caused George to lose his job. He treated his step-children so harshly that Elizabeth left him and moved into a rented house, again taking in boarders for income so as not to deplete what was left of her meagre savings from the sale of the house in Rhein. Johnnie and Reinhold, her youngest sons, found odd jobs to contribute to the family's sustenance.

In 1939, when Canada declared war on Germany, Reinhold went back to Rhein. Prime Minister William Lyon Mackenzie King did not institute conscription, but Johnnie enlisted voluntarily. Lillian and Alvina's paycheques helped with the rent, but that wasn't enough, so Elizabeth found employment in a garment factory, sewing pockets on soldier's uniform pants.

Back in Rhein, Henry married Helen, Sarah married Fred, and each couple had one daughter. Reinhold and Johnnie married women with the same first name, Mary. Johnnie's Mary was an English war bride. In Winnipeg, Alvina and Lillian married men with the same first name, Bill.

Elizabeth felt a pull to return to Saskatchewan. She shared a suite in Yorkton with her sister. She never uttered the name of George or spoke of that brief chapter in her life. On her dresser in a little silver frame was a black-and-white photo of Heinrich. She told her grandchildren she was lucky that he had married her because he was good-looking and she was plain.

At the age of seventy, she became eligible for the $40-per-month Old Age Security Pension, and moved into seniors' subsidized housing. She treasured her little apartment and her independence.

After spending a night in the bathtub, unable to climb out, she was placed in a nursing home. That picture of Heinrich, her eternally young and handsome husband who died in 1919 from the Spanish Flu, the father of her six children, was on her bedside table.

She whispered, "*Mein Gott*, take me to be with Heinrich" before she breathed her last breath at the age of ninety-one.

Elizabeth II

In Regina, Saskatchewan, Elizabeth lives with her husband Josh and their two children in a two-story three bedroom/three bath semi-detached home. She is the namesake of her paternal great-grandmother, a German immigrant from Russia. It has been three generations and more than one hundred years since her great-grandparents homesteaded in Rhein.

Elizabeth and Josh have one son and one daughter, just as they planned, followed by Josh's vasectomy. Elizabeth is the creative type, a freelance writer and editor for a small publisher. Her children's picture book, *Mommy + Daddy + 2 Kids,* the first in a series, has just been released. Josh is a practical guy, a tax auditor for the Canada Revenue Agency. He tinkers with vintage cars in his spare time. The children are in French immersion, hockey, and rhythmic gymnastics.

Their day-to-day lives are much the same as other suburban families raised by parents who championed the benefits of a post-secondary education. They make monthly payments on a whopping mortgage and two vehicles, a Honda Civic and a Subaru. A 1949 Mercury Coupe is in the garage.

In late February 2020, news of the Novel Coronavirus reaches Regina. On March 11, The World Health Organization declares Covid-19 a pandemic.

Regina Leader-Post March 13: "Saskatchewan's first presumptive case of Covid-19 has been detected. The person experiencing symptoms is a Saskatoon resident in their sixties who had recently travelled to Egypt. Saskatchewan's chief medical officer is confident the province's first presumptive case of Covid-19 has been contained, though he warned it's unlikely to be the last and urged the public to prepare for 'tough decisions'... Dr. Shahab had two central messages for the general public. He asked residents to seek testing if they develop symptoms and to help prevent transmission by maintaining social distance."

Social distance is a new concept, but Elizabeth and Josh adjust, and remind the children of new protocols at school.

On March 18, Saskatchewan declares a state of emergency and restricts gatherings. Certain businesses are ordered to close, while others must limit capacity.

Both Josh and Elizabeth now work from home. Thank goodness their family trip to Cancun was during the February school break, before travellers were required to self-isolate for fourteen days.

In-class learning is suspended on March 20. Elizabeth takes a leave-of-absence to help the children with remote learning.

With summer camps cancelled, they purchase a trampoline and an above-ground swimming pool. They tent for two weeks in the Qu'Appelle Valley while Josh is on vacation.

Just before the so-called safe return to in-classroom learning in September, Josh develops a cough and fever, most likely just the flu or a cold. To be on the safe side, he goes for a Covid test. A nurse calls in forty-eight hours to say that he tested positive. She asks for names of contacts in an effort to trace the source.

"The nurse said I have to self-isolate for two weeks," he tells Elizabeth. "I'll stay downstairs."

There's a hide-a-bed, TV, and bathroom in the basement. They communicate by cell phone. Elizabeth opens the door and sets his meals on the top step.

On Elizabeth's thirtieth birthday, Josh's symptoms worsen. She arranges a babysitter. Both wearing masks, she drives him to the hospital outpatient department.

"I packed an overnight bag for you," she says.

"I brought my iPad just in case."

They air kiss good-bye from behind masks. She is not allowed to go in.

"I won't be long, hopefully, if there isn't a line-up."

After four hours in the parking lot, she receives a text. "They're admitting me. We'll celebrate your birthday when I come home. Promise. Sorry."

They FaceTime every evening. Josh mostly listens because of his shortness of breath. After he is put on a ventilator with a mask, a care aide holds the iPad.

On October 30, Elizabeth shops for costumes at Walmart after school. She is in a foul mood and could use a pick-me-up, or at least a distraction.

The kids try on their costumes as soon as they get home to show Josh on FaceTime.

"Look at me, Daddy! I'm Spiderman."

Josh tries to nod.

"I'm Tinkerbell. We're going trick-or-treating tomorrow, but Mommy says only on our block this year because of the pandemic."

After the children are in bed, a nurse calls to tell Elizabeth that Josh will have to be intubated. "He wants to talk to you."

Josh pushes his mask aside. "If I don't make it...." He gasps for breath.

Elizabeth is sobbing.

The nurse puts his mask back on. After a few breaths, he pushes it aside again. "The kids..."

Elizabeth interrupts him. "You're coming home again, Josh."

He struggles to speak.

The nurse, tears in her eyes, repeats what Josh was trying to say. "He said he wishes he could see the kids grow up."

Elizabeth shouts, "You have to come home!"

Sleepless, Elizabeth prays for her husband's recovery. She hasn't attended church since their wedding, can't remember the last time she prayed, and doesn't know if she believes in a higher power.

She calls Josh the next morning, bracing herself to sound hopeful.

A neighbour takes the kids trick-or-treating after school. They come home with candy spilling out of their plastic pumpkins, and gorge themselves until Elizabeth puts the pumpkins out of reach on a high shelf. She allows them to wear their costumes to bed, insists they brush their teeth, and tucks them in. Her son is clasping a rubber spider. She doesn't know about the superstition that seeing a spider on Hallowe'en Eve is a sign that a loved one's spirit is watching over you.

On the eve of Hallowe'en 2020, while Tinkerbell and Spiderman are asleep, Josh dies at the age of thirty-four.

At 10 p.m., Elizabeth's cell phone rings. An ICU doctor says, "I'm calling to inform you that your husband, Josh, just died. I'm so sorry."

Elizabeth presses "End call" and collapses. She lies flat on her stomach on the cool hardwood floor, her head turned to one side. At first she is silent. Numb. Then she wails. The sounds she makes are those of a woman on the TV news, a mother in a hijab discovering her child's body in bits after another bombing in Aleppo. It is the death wail. Eventually it settles into moaning.

Elizabeth is a thirty-year-old widow with two children. Now she knows for sure there is no God.

This story was inspired by the death of the author's grandfather, Heinrich Weinmeister, on Oct. 31, 1919 in Rhein, Saskatchewan, from the after-effects of the Spanish Flu.

PARENTAL WISDOM

Moni Brar

my father wipes the cobwebs
from his eyes
straightens his turban
watches the red numbers
tick upwards on the tv screen
while through the window
a hummingbird hangs midair

mother picks stones
from mung beans
rinses aged dirt from rice
murmurs wahegurus
to keep the evil at bay
wonders how the village
will survive this

father reassures her
reminds her
of the monsoons and floods,
the droughts and dengue,
the cholera and smallpox
tells her it's a gift to feel whole
to see the world unhinge, then mend

CONTRIBUTORS' BIOS

Ruth "Reno" Anderson is a fierce Jesus follower. After a varied career, from English teacher to newspaper editor to international relief manager to chaplain, she loves to write, travel, read, paint, and walk her dogs. Reno and her husband, aka "The Faster Pastor," have travelled all over the world, but they currently live in Delisle.

Regina author **Byrna Barclay** has published twelve books of fiction, the most recent being *House of the White Elephant* and *Second Cousin Once Removed*. She was awarded the Saskatchewan Order of Merit in 2005. "Dinner with Andrew Cuomo" is from a new collection of short stories, her first attempt at humour, an accident of fiction.

Carla Barkman is a family physician with an interest in narrative medicine. She divides her time between Regina, where she is completing a BA (English), and the north. Her poems can be found in various literary journals and anthologies.

Poetry editor **Courtney Bates-Hardy** is the author of *House of Mystery* (2016) and a chapbook, *Sea Foam* (2013). Her poems can be found in *Room, Carousel,* and *This Magazine,* among others. They have been featured in *Imaginarium 4: Best Canadian Speculative Poetry* and are forthcoming in *Best Canadian Poetry 2021.* She lives in Regina with her partner and their cat.

Elena Bentley is a disabled poet, writer, editor, and book reviewer from Clavet. She is of Métis and mixed ancestry. In 2018, Elena completed an MA in English literature at the University of Toronto. Her poetry has been published in *untethered, Arc* and *spring* magazines. She is the newly appointed poetry editor for *untethered.*

Belinda Betker's first poetry collection, *Phases*, was a 2020 finalist for two Saskatchewan Book Awards. Her work is also published in various anthologies, literary journals, chapbooks, and online. She lives in Saskatoon with her Australian wife and their rescue dog, a springer-spaniel/terrier cross. Belinda loves getting lost – in any good book, and in any new or second-hand bookstore – anytime, anywhere.

Rita Bouvier is author of three collections of poetry. *nakamowin'sa for the seasons* (Thistledown Press, 2015) was a Saskatchewan Book Awards 2016 winner of the Aboriginal Peoples' Writing Award. Her poetry has appeared in literary journals and anthologies, musicals and television productions, and has been translated into Spanish, German and Cree-Michif of her home community of saskitawak— Île-à-la-Crosse.

The recent loss of her life partner and best friend has made Covid-19 a true trial for Big River poet **Carla Braidek**. Her home in the boreal forest provides isolation and comfort but is much more enjoyable when shared by others. Carla's previous publications include poetry books *A Map in My Blood* and *Carrying the Sun*.

Born in northern India, **Moni Brar** now lives in Calgary on unsurrendered territories of the Treaty 7 region and Syilx Okanagan Nation. Her writing explores the interrelation of time, place and identity in the immigrant experience, diasporan guilt, intergenerational trauma, and colonization. She believes art contains the possibility of healing. Her work appears in *PRISM*, *Passages North*, *Prairie Fire*, *Hobart*, and others.

Bev Brenna is a Saskatoon poet and teacher, previously published in *Contemporary Verse II*, *Dandelion*, *Grain*, *The Auteur*, *The Prairie Journal*, *Trout*, and *Zygote*, with recent work in the *Life of Pie* anthology and *Resistance*. She has also raised orphan lambs, jumped out of planes, and written fourteen books for children and young adults www.beverleybrenna.com. And she's married to Dwayne.

Dwayne Brenna has been a school bus driver, a baseball poet, a hired hand, a Doctor of Philosophy, a carpenter, a university professor, a carwash attendant, a disk jockey, an actor at the Stratford Festival of Canada, a tour guide, an award-winning novelist, and a lumberyard lackey. He lives and works in Saskatoon.

Sharon Butala has spent most of her eighty years in Saskatchewan but now lives in Calgary. She has published twenty books and will have an essay collection out this fall. She's had bestsellers and near-flops, and won many prizes, though not the biggies, where she remains an also-ran. She's a member of the Saskatchewan Order of Merit and the Order of Canada.

CC Corbett is a Prince Albert-based emerging writer who was raised in various communities across north-central Saskatchewan. She holds a Master's degree in Education. She has written novels, children's books, poetry, songs, and creative nonfiction to both entertain and reconcile life's challenges. Her poetry has previously been published in *spring* and *The Society.* This is her first fiction publication.

Chelsea Coupal's first poetry collection, *Sedley* (Coteau, 2018), was shortlisted for three Saskatchewan Book Awards and selected by Chapters Indigo for an Indigo Exclusive edition. She has won the City of Regina Writing Award and been shortlisted for *CV2*'s Young Buck Poetry Prize. Her work has appeared in *Arc, Event, Grain* and *Best Canadian Poetry*, among other publications.

Joan Crate lives in Calgary and the Okanagan but visits Saskatchewan when it's not winter. Her poems reflect life in isolation while trying to recover from the devastating loss of her life partner of 38 years. She is the author of three books of poetry, two novels, hundreds of poems, a few stories and a dabble of essays.

Robert Currie of Moose Jaw is the author most recently of *One-Way Ticket.* He served as Saskatchewan's third poet laureate and is a recipient of the Lieutenant-Governor's Award for Lifetime Achievement in the Arts. He has been a member of the SWG since 1973 and would like that to continue; so he persists in physical distancing and wearing a mask.

Saskatoon's **Amanda Dawson** is a writer and educator who grew up in rural Alberta, where she spent most of her time reading books and stargazing. Her work has appeared in *Drunk Monkeys, spring, The Molotov Cocktail*, and others. She is currently an MFA in Writing candidate at the University of Saskatchewan. This is her first published work in an anthology.

Deidra Suwanee Dees follows Muscogee stompdance traditions and serves as director/tribal archivist at Poarch Band of Creek Indians in Alabama. She teaches Native American Studies at University of South Alabama in Mobile. A Cornell and Harvard graduate, she wrote her dissertation on Muscogee Education Movement. She writes poetry in her head, sketching verses on McDonald's bags at traffic lights.

Myrna Garanis is an Edmonton-based, Saskatchewan-raised poet and essayist. With Ivan Sundal, she edited and published the anthology *Life of Pie: Prairie Poems and Prose* in 2020.

Beth Goobie is the author of twenty-five books. A new collection of poetry, *Lookin' for Joy*, is due out with Exile Editions in 2022. It was gratefully written with the assistance of a SK Arts grant. Beth lives in Saskatoon.

Janet Hainstock doubles as a pirate as she swipes ideas for her writing from the antics of her children and grandchildren. She has one anecdote published in the As Kids See It section of the September 2019 *Reader's Digest*. This is her first poem to be published. She lives in Moose Jaw.

Louise Bernice Halfe, a former Saskatchewan poet laureate, is Canada's latest parliamentary poet laureate. Her new volume of poems, *awasis, kinky and dishevelled*, was published this spring by Brick Books. She lives near Saskatoon.

Madonna Hamel was born in Dawson Creek, B.C. She lives in Val Marie. She's been a writer-broadcaster and documentary producer for CBC Radio, a book reviewer for *The Globe & Mail*, a weekly columnist, a touring monologist – and a backup singer. She recently won *Prairie Fire*'s creative nonfiction prize and is working on a novel.

Regina poet **gillian harding-russell**'s books include *Uninterrupted* (Ekstasis Editions, 2020) and *In Another Air* (Radiant Press, 2018). She completed her PhD at the University of Saskatchewan – from which she learned, if nothing else, to sieve through life's detritus. In 2016, *Making Sense* won Exile's Gwendolyn MacEwen chapbook award. A chapbook, *Megrim* (The Alfred Gustav Press), will be released this spring.

Jason Heit was raised on his family farm in west-central Saskatchewan; his writing is inspired by rural Saskatchewan, its people, and their stories. Heit's first book, *Kaidenberg's Best Sons* (Coteau Books, 2019; Guernica Editions, 2020), won two Saskatchewan Book Awards. He lives near Pike Lake with his wife, Jacqueline, and their children.

Raye Hendrikson, who calls Regina home, feels that Saskatchewan's prairie terrain allows her to breathe. Her poetry explores the mysteries and curiosities of science and nature, of our minds and spirits, and of relationships. In addition to publications in literary magazines and anthologies, she is the author of *Five Red Sentries*, which was shortlisted for two 2020 Saskatchewan Book Awards.

dee Hobsbawn-Smith, a former equestrian, basketball player, chef and journalist, is a poet, fictionista, award-winning essayist, runner, quilter, gardener, orchid grower, and locavore. She has two wonderful sons, an MFA in Writing, and an MA in Literature. Her eighth book, *Bread & Water: Essays*, will be published by University of Regina Press in Fall 2021. dee lives rurally, west of Saskatoon.

Judit Katalin Hollos is a Hungarian poet, playwright, translator and journalist living in Budapest. She studied playwriting and screenwriting in Hungary and Swedish literature and language in Vaxjö, Sweden. Her short stories and poems have been featured in literary magazines and anthologies. Her first play received a reading in Glasgow. Her first poetry chapbook, *Nacreous*, was published in 2020.

Delane Just lives in Saskatoon and is a current student in the MFA in Writing program at the University of Saskatchewan. She has had work appear in *In Medias Res* and *The University of Saskatchewan Undergraduate Research Journal*. She is also the coordinator for the River Volta Reading Series.

Holly Keeler is a physiotherapist working as a team manager in long-term care. She has published poems in *spring*, *The Fieldstone Review*, and the forthcoming anthology *Within These Lines* by the Obsessors Group. She was raised on a farm near her current home, Saskatoon, where she lives with her dog, cats, husband and three adult daughters.

Tanisha Khan was born in Bangladesh and grew up in Toronto. She likes to think she has many homes, her most recent one being Regina. Her writing explores the elegiac and fractured workings of memory through the lens of fantastical fiction. She is currently completing her MFA in Creative Writing at the University of Oregon. This story is her first publication.

Karen Klassen was on the island of Saipan when the pandemic struck. She plans to stay and windsurf in the tropics until the world is free to travel again and she can return home to Victoria, BC. Much of Karen's writing is inspired by her childhood and family. Her work can be found in a number of anthologies and journals.

Miriam Körner is an award-winning children's writer and illustrator, whose work reflects on our (lost) connection to the natural world. Originally from Germany, she lives with her partner and their sled dogs in northern Saskatchewan, where land and people inspire her writing and way of life. She is currently working on her third novel.

Regina poet **Judith Krause** is a long-time member of the provincial writing community. A former Saskatchewan poet laureate, she's the author of five collections and a collaborative chapbook. Recent publications include poems in *Grain*, the League of Canadian Poets anthology *Heartwood* and the forthcoming anthologies, *Resistance* (University of Regina Press) and *Best Canadian Poetry 2021* (Biblioasis).

Bestselling author **Alice Kuipers** has published twelve books for children and young adults, and she regularly shares books she loves on CTV in Saskatoon, where she lives with her four children. Her work is published in thirty-six countries. She's also co-founder of the non-profit @OneSmallStepSk. Find her here: www.alicekuipers.com, @alicekuipersbookclub

Allison Kydd of Indian Head is a longstanding member of the SWG who loves writing retreats, when the world is not locked down. She's published two books: *Emily via the Greyhound Bus*, a novella (Thistledown, 2012) and a historical novel, *Few and Far*. (Stonehouse, 2017). She writes a newspaper column called "Local Heroes" and has won prizes for short stories.

Katherine Lawrence is the author of four poetry collections including *Stay*, a young adult novel-in-verse. A new collection of poems, *Black Umbrella*, is forthcoming (Turnstone Press). Originally from Hamilton, Katherine has lived in Saskatoon for over thirty-five years. She is a former writer-in-residence with Saskatoon Public Library and holds an MFA in Creative Writing from the University of Saskatchewan.

Anne Lazurko is an award-winning novelist, a no-awards farmer, and a sometimes poet. Growing up in the microcosm of tiny-town Saskatchewan was excellent fodder for exploring character and story. Her new novel, *What is Written on the Tongue*, is forthcoming from ECW Press. Anne now lives and farms near Weyburn.

Shelley A. Leedahl is a former Saskatchewanian now living in Ladysmith, B.C. Her books include poetry and short story collections, novels, nonfiction, and children's literature, and she frequently writes book reviews. Leedahl's recent titles include *The Moon Watched It All* and *I Wasn't Always Like This*. *Go* – a new poetry collection – will be out with Radiant Press in 2022. writersunion.ca/member/shellya-leedahl

Alison Lohans has called Regina home since 1976, after growing up in California, then living in B.C. She's published twenty-six books – picture books up through mature YA novels – with Canadian and international presses. She also writes short fiction, poetry, and creative nonfiction. Alison has taught writing, done some editing, won awards, and was writer-in-residence at Regina Public Library.

Jeanette Lynes is the author of two novels and seven collections of poetry. Her third novel is forthcoming from HarperCollins Canada in 2022. Jeanette directs the MFA in Writing at the University of Saskatchewan. In her spare time, she continues to work on a collection of personal essays and collects vintage aprons when the thrift shops are not locked down.

Prose and managing editor **Dave Margoshes** lives near Saskatoon. He's published twenty books of fiction, nonfiction and poetry, and been an editor on newspapers, magazines and of books.

Mary Maxwell's writing in three genres, including a chapbook and a book of poems, has been published across Canada. Her employment in four provinces ranged from a nurse at a poultry plant to an investigator for the provincial Ombudsman. Of all the places she's travelled, her favourites are the wilds of Canada and Tasmania. She lives in Saskatoon.

Shannon McConnell is a writer, educator, and musician originally from Vancouver, now living in Kingston. Her poetry and fiction have appeared in *untethered, Louden Singletree, Rat's Ass Review*, and more. She holds an MFA in writing and an MA in history from the University of Saskatchewan. In 2020, her debut poetry collection, *The Burden of Gravity*, was published by Caitlin Press.

Caitlin McCullam-Arnal grew up in Loree, Ontario, but now lives in Ravenscrag, SK, with her husband and nine rescue animals. In 2020, she was awarded the John V. Hicks Scholarship to attend Sage Hill Writing's fiction course. She draws inspiration from things that piss her off and make her smile. She's been published in *Transition*. This is her first anthology.

Melanie McFarlane is a novelist, amateur potter, poet and claims adjuster. She has a Creative Writing certificate from the University of Calgary and is working on the final two classes for her BA at Athabasca University. She has six novels published and her poetry can be found in *Transition* magazine. She has resided in Moose Jaw for over thirty years.

Bronwen McRae is a Saskatchewan lifer, currently residing in Saskatoon. Her work has appeared in literary magazines and is forthcoming in three anthologies including *Within These Lines* which is a collaborative effort of her poetry group, The Obsessors. Bronwen looks forward to taking up her bass clarinet and rejoining her Saskatoon Community Band mates once the pandemic is over.

Lynda Monahan lives in the pines of north central Saskatchewan. She recently had double cataract surgery and the world has suddenly come into focus. She had no idea that trees had that many leaves. There are poems to write about everything. She has authored four poetry collections and been writer-in-residence at the Cuelenaere Library and Victoria Hospital in Prince Albert.

The prairie landscape and its people have inspired **Helen Mourre**'s three short fiction collections: *Landlocked*, *What's Come Over Her*, and *To Everything A Season*. More recently, she has transitioned into writing creative nonfiction and has completed a manuscript entitled *The Renaissance of a Prairie Pilgrim*. Helen Mourre lives in Rosetown.

Lorri Neilsen Glenn's most recent book is *Following the River: Traces of Red River Women*, an award-winning hybrid work about her Ininiwak and Métis grandmothers. Author and editor of fourteen titles of nonfiction and poetry, Lorri served as Halifax Poet Laureate, is Professor Emerita (Mount Saint Vincent University) and now teaches in The University of King's College MFA program.

Karen Nye worked in the medical, policing, business, academic, media and non-profit sectors while raising three sons in Lumsden as a single mom. Tired, retired and now re-inspired, this emerging poet was an apprentice in the SWG mentorship program and attended Sage Hill Writing Experience. Her poetry can be found in *A Gift of the Prairie*, *spring* and *line dance*.

Aliza Prodaniuk is a graduate of McMaster University and currently lives in Dundas, Ontario. Her writing has been published in various magazines and journals, exploring anything from science, travel, interpersonal relationships, and beyond! She's currently happy to have time to focus on writing while learning alongside others in the MFA in Writing program at the University of Saskatchewan.

Medrie Purdham lives in Regina and teaches at the University of Regina. Her poems have been anthologized in *Best Canadian Poetry*, long-listed for the CBC Poetry Prize and was runner-up in *Arc* magazine's poem-of-the-year contest in 2019. She won the 2015 City of Regina Writing Award. Her first book of poetry, *Little Housewolf*, has just been published by Véhicule Press.

Lloyd Ratzlaff has authored three books of literary nonfiction (Thistledown Press), edited a collection of seniors' writings (READ Saskatoon), been a columnist for *Prairie Messenger Catholic Journal*, and contributed to literary anthologies. He's taught writing classes at the University of Saskatchewan and Western Development Museum, and served on the boards of several writing organizations. He lives and writes in Saskatoon.

Paula Jane Remlinger's poetry has appeared in journals across Canada and in a number of anthologies. Her first book, *This Hole Called January* (Thistledown, 2019) won the 2020 Saskatchewan Book Award for Poetry. She lives in Beaver Creek, where she edits and writes a variety of genres for children and adults.

Jill Robinson, a former Saskatoon resident, lives and writes in Banff, though she recently served as the 2020-21 writer-in-residence at the Regina Public Library. She has published four collections of stories and a novel, and is presently working on a collection of creative nonfiction essays.

William Robertson lives in Saskatoon where he recently retired from teaching in the Indian Teacher Education Program at the University of Saskatchewan. He's heard that writing is hard, but changing tires all day is harder, and dirtier. So are the oil rigs. His latest book of poetry is *Decoys*.

Jenny Ryan of Saskatoon is a full-time librarian, a part-time comedian, and an occasional poet. During the pandemic, she has not completed any puzzles, nor has she has learned any instruments, but she has become quite prolific on Twitter. She has previously been published in *Grain*, *paperplates*, *Fieldstone Review*, and was the inaugural winner of CBC's Canada Writes competition.

Brenda Schmidt is the author of five books of poetry and a book of essays. Her work is included in *The Best of the Best Canadian Poetry in English: Tenth Anniversary Edition*. She was the seventh Saskatchewan poet laureate. She lives on the dry side of a hill in central west Saskatchewan where she's exploring the poetry of xeriscaping.

Glen Sorestad is a long-time poet from Saskatoon whose poems have been published in many countries and translated into eight languages. Two of his more than twenty books of poetry are bilingual volumes, the English/Italian *Selected Poems from Dancing Birches* (2020) and *A Thief of Impeccable Taste* (2011). He was Saskatchewan's first poet laureate – the first such provincial post in Canada.

Tracy Stevens is a Métis woman who lives in Regina. She cheers for the underdog, is intrigued by true crime stories, and is attracted to bad-ass characters. She earned a college certificate in communications. Tracy is finding her voice. This is her first published story.

Shayna Stock grew up on the shores of Lake Huron and now lives in Regina/ Treaty 4. She writes about queer lineage and love, gender and sexuality, and connection to place. She has performed spoken word across the country, and her poetry has been published in *Grain* magazine. This is her first publication in an anthology.

Saskatoon's **Leona Theis** writes novels, short stories and personal essays. She's the author of three books, most recently the novel-in-stories *If Sylvie Had Nine Lives*, winner of the John V. Hicks manuscript award. Her essays have won awards from the CBC, *Prairie Fire* magazine, and elsewhere. Her current dream is to do an extended walking tour somewhere on the Prairies.

Michael Trussler writes poetry, short stories and creative nonfiction. His anthologized (often experimental), work engages with the beauty and violence of the twentieth and twenty-first centuries. His short fiction collection, *Encounters*, won Saskatchewan Book of the Year in 2006. This essay is part of *The Sunday Book*, a memoir that will be published by Palimpsest in 2022.

Maureen Ulrich is an author/playwright/retired teacher from southeast Saskatchewan. Coteau Books released her YA Jessie Mac Hockey series (*Power Plays, Face Off, Breakaway*) 2007-2012. Maureen has relaunched the series with Wood Dragon Books. When she isn't writing, Maureen enjoys attending football, baseball, and hockey games, reading, and riding her motorcycle.

Bernadette Wagner, an award-winning Regina writer and instructor, has edited more than thirty books, chapbooks, and magazines. She loves to sing and garden, cook and preserve, teach and learn, as well as play with words and language. In 2021, she studied with Zen meditation and writing teacher Natalie Goldberg, and started jalapeno and sweet pepper seeds indoors.

Jayne Melville Whyte advocates community development toward fulfilling lives with and for people with mental illness and other disabilities. She contributes regularly to *Transition* (Canadian Mental Health Association Saskatchewan). She's the author of *Pivot Points: A Fragmented History of Mental Health* in Saskatchewan (CMHA, 2012). Jayne lives in Regina Housing.

Prince Albert's **Denise Wilkinson** works as a teacher, which she loves because her students are awesome and the income supports her writing habit. She has an MFA in Writing, an amazing collection of books, and never enough time to read or write. While she loves yoga, dancing, and meditating, her favourite is spending time with her husband and two sons.

P. J. Worrell is a Saskatchewan farm girl and social worker, living in Swift Current. Her debut collection of short fiction, *Proudflesh*, was a finalist for Saskatchewan Book of the Year and First Book. Other stories have been included in anthologies. Themes in her writing are disappointment and loss. She is working on a novel and a non-fiction manuscript.

Michelle Yeo has taught kindergarten and graduate students, student teachers and professors. She's taught in the pool and at the school. She believes in the power of fermentation and digging in the dirt. She lives with a daughter and a dog in Calgary. She has previously been published in *FreeFall*. This is her first anthology contribution.